Mathew Carey

Atlas Minimus

A new Set of Pocket Maps of various Empires, Kingdoms, and States

Mathew Carey

Atlas Minimus
A new Set of Pocket Maps of various Empires, Kingdoms, and States

ISBN/EAN: 9783337174941

Printed in Europe, USA, Canada, Australia, Japan

Cover: Foto ©Andreas Hilbeck / pixelio.de

More available books at **www.hansebooks.com**

ATLAS MINIMUS:

OR, A NEW SET OF

POCKET MAPS,

Of various EMPIRES, KINGDOMS, and STATES,

WITH

Geographical Extracts relative to each.

===

DRAWN AND ENGRAVED,

By J. GIBSON,

===

FROM THE BEST AUTHORITIES.

A NEW EDITION,

REVISED, CORRECTED, AND IMPROVED.

PHILADELPHIA,
PRINTED FOR *MATHEW CAREY*,
No. 118, MARKET-STREET.
April 14, 1798.

PREFACE.

THOUGH this work, which contains a comprehenfive view of the feveral parts of the globe, with hiftorical extracts refpecting each map, was intended to give young gentlemen and ladies a general idea of geography; it may likewife be of fervice to thofe of more years and experience; fince it is impoffible for the mind, however capacious, to remember precifely all the divifions, and fubdivifions, of the feveral ftates and kingdoms in the world; and it will be more acceptable, we prefume, as no other epitome of this kind has been offered to the public that is fo convenient for the pocket, or which contains the many modern difcoveries with which the fcience has been enriched.

Nothing need be faid in favour of this ftudy; almoft every one is acquainted with its ufefulnefs and excellency, and fees how effential it is, towards forming the character of the fine gentleman and agreeable companion.

The Editor having publifhed an Atlas of the United States, intended to accompany this work, has not introduced here any ftate maps, and therefore refers the reader to the above publication, in which thofe maps are given on a larger fcale than any in this collection.

INDEX.

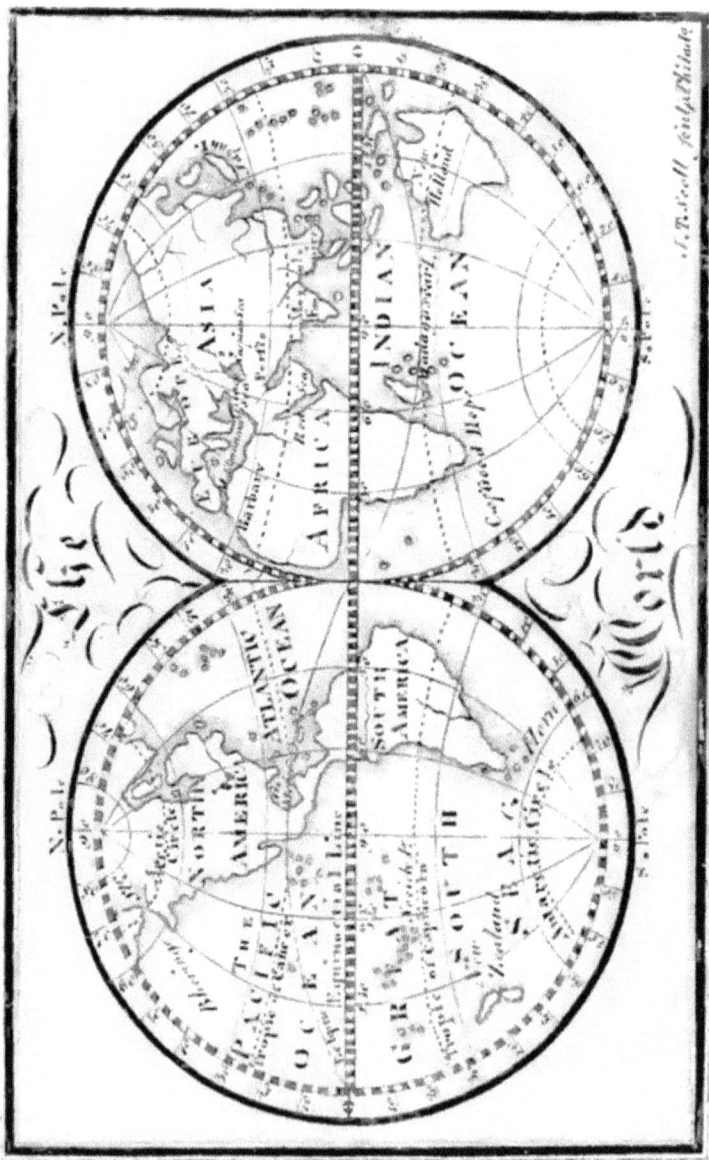

The World

THE GLOBE OF THE WORLD.

THE World we inhabit, which confifts of Land and Water, is well delineated on Maps, either drawn or printed on Paper. Of thefe fome are *general*, and others *particular*. A general map is that which reprefents whole Kingdoms, States, and Empires, and even fometimes the World at large ; fuch are the collection of maps contained in this volume. A particular map is that which reprefents only fome fmall part of a large kingdom or province, but defcribes every particular city, town, or village, it contains.

As the furface of the earth, on which we dwell, is made up of two parts, land and water, each of thefe elements have their various parts and fub-divifions, which are as varioufly defcribed on maps. The land is called either an ifland, a continent, a peninfula, an ifthmus, a promontory, or a cape.——An ifland is a country, or portion of land, encompaffed about with the fea, as Great Britain, Ireland, &c. A continent, properly fo called, is an extenfive fpace of land, on which many ftates and kingdoms are joined, and not feparated from each other by the fea. Such are Europe, Afia, &c. This is fometimes called the main land. A peninfula is a part of land encompaffed with water, or which is almoft an ifland : fuch is the Morea which joins to Greece, Denmark which joins to Germany, &c. An ifthmus is a very narrow neck of land between two feas, joining a peninfula to a continent. A promontory is a hill, or point of land ftretching out into the fea, and is often called a cape. A coaft, or fhore, is all that land that borders upon the fea, whe-

B   ther

ther it be in iflands or continents. The land is divided or diftinguifhed from the fea in maps by a thick fhadow made of fmall fhort ftrokes, to reprefent the fhores or coafts, whether of continents or iflands. Kingdoms, or provinces, are divided from each other by a row of fingle points, and thefe are often painted or ftained with different colours. Cities or great towns are made on maps like little houfes, with a fmall circle in the middle of them; but fmaller towns or villages are marked only by fuch a fmall circle. Mountains are imitated in the form of little rifing hillocks, and forefts are reprefented by a collection of little trees. The names of villages are wrote in a running hand, the names of cities in a Roman character, and provinces in large capitals.—The water is divided into rivers or feas. A river is a ftream of water, which has ufually its beginning from a fmall fpring or fountain; but the word fea implies a larger quantity of water, and is diftinguifhed into lakes, gulfs, bays, creeks, ftraits, or the ocean. The ocean or the main fea, is a vaft fpreading collection of water, which is not divided by lands. A lake is a large expanfe of water inclofed all round with land. A gulph is a part of the fea that is almoft encompaffed with land, or that runs up a great way into the land. A ftrait is a narrow part of the ocean lying between two fhores, whereby two feas are joined together. Rocks are reprefented in maps like little pointed things, fticking up fharp in the fea; and fands or fhelves by a great heap of little points placed in the fhape of thofe fands they are fuppofed to reprefent.

EUROPE.

IS situate between 10° W. and 65° E. Longitude, and between 36° and 72° N. Latitude, being bounded by the Frozen Ocean on the north, by Asia on the east, by the Mediterranean on the south, which divides it from Africa, and by the Atlantic Ocean on the west. The islands in the Mediterranean Sea are Ivica, subject to Spain, as is likewise Majorca and Minorca. Corsica was formerly subject to Genoa, but became a free state under the brave Paoli, who has since been driven out of the country by the French; it is now, however, subject to the crown of England. Sardinia is subject to its own king, and Sicily to the king of Naples. The islands of the Archipelago, together with that of Candia, own the grand Turk for their master. The islands of Great Britain, &c. are mentioned at the bottom of the map; those of the Baltic, the Adriatic and Ionian seas are inconsiderable. Europe is not nearly so extensive as either Asia or Africa, though it infinitely surpasses them in many particulars. It lies entirely within the temperate zone, except a small part of Norway and Muscovy; and hence it is not exposed to those excessive heats of the summer, or piercing cold of the winter, which some parts of the globe feel at the various seasons of the year. It does not abound in those luxurious ornaments, gold and diamonds, nor is it pestered with those ravenous beasts of prey, which make travelling over the deserts of Africa, and some other parts, so dangerous to those who are obliged to venture on such inhospitable sands. Here are no leopards, hyænas, tigers, lions, &c. but such as are kept confined

for

EUROPE.

for the infpection of the curious. It produces corn, wine, and the moft delicious fruits, with every thing that is neceffary for the purpofes of human life. If it is fmaller than Afia or Africa, it is much more populous and better cultivated than either of them. There are in Europe none of thofe barren and frightful waftes which are met with in other parts of the world; but inftead of them large and populous cities, ftrong and magnificently built, with beautiful villages interfperfed. Europe is the feat of the arts and fciences, where they are carried to the higheft pitch of perfection, and where the natives of every part of the globe refort to, as to the fchool of wifdom and humanity. The Europeans are white, and better made than the Africans or Afiatics who are many of them fo very unpolifhed as hardly to refemble the human fpecies, owing principally to the want of the knowledge of the arts, and the advantages of fociety. It muft indeed be confeffed, that in fome parts of Europe, even in thefe enlightened days, there are ftill inhabitants in the northern regions, who are as little civilized, and as much unacquainted with the fciences, as many of the Africans. The fouthern part of Europe is much more popnlous than the northern, where the cold is fome parts of the year fo great as make it very uncomfortable to the inhabitants, who frequently emigrate to the fouth, to live under warmer and more fertile climates. Europe contains about 4,456,065 fquare miles ; the habitable parts of the world in the other quarters are eftimated at 36,666,806 fquare miles.

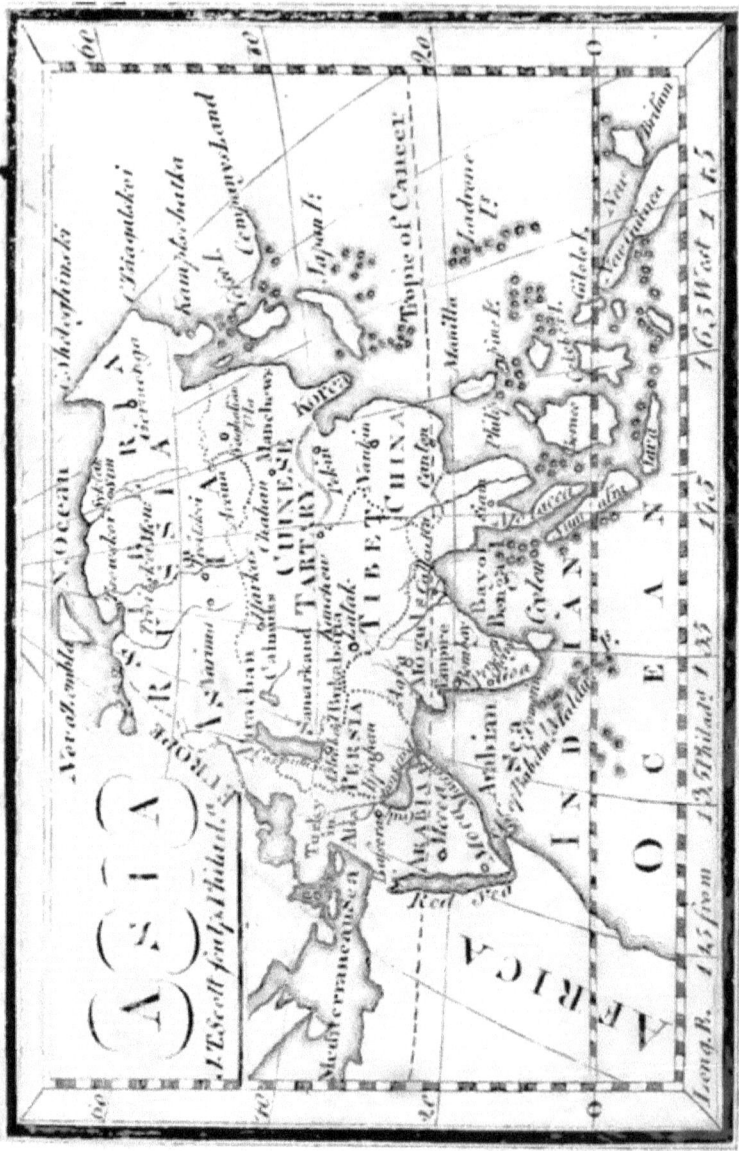

ASIA.

THE continent of Asia is situate between 25° and 148° of east longitude, and between the equator and 72° of north latitude. It is bounded by the Frozen Ocean on the north, by the Pacific Ocean on the east, by the Indian Ocean on the south, and on the west by the Red Sea, the Levant, Archipelago, Hellespont, Propontis, Bosphorus, the Black-Sea, the Palus Meotis, river Don, and the line drawn from that river to the river Tobol, and from thence to the river Oby, which falls into the Frozen Ocean.—In Asia is the Caspian Sea, which is two thousand miles in circumference; and lake Aral, which has not long been known to the Europeans, is at least half that extent; besides several other very considerable lakes. The principal rivers are the Tigris and Euphrates, the Ganges and Indus. The highest mountains are Ararat, on which Noah's ark rested after the deluge, Horeb and Sinai, Taurus, and Caucasus. This quarter of the world, as it is called, is much larger than either Europe or Africa, and man is said to have received his first existence here. Though arts and sciences undoubtedly first took their rise in Egypt, yet it is certain that they made a very early appearance in Asia, from whence all the considerable modes of religion had their first beginning. There are still many Asiatics, who maintain their ancient tenets, which they tell you have been preserved in their utmost purity above a hundred thousand years. Cities were first built in Asia, and empires founded — The governments of Asia are monarchical, and divided among several sovereigns, who are reckoned to consist

of

A S I A.

of feven emperors, thirty kings, befides petty princes, and the rajahs of India, who are very numerous. As to the extent of their religions, the Chriftian is but fmall when compared with the Mahometan, which comprehends one third of Afia; but the Pagan is much more extenfive than the Mahometan. Befides thefe, fome pretend there is the natural religion, whofe number, like thofe of the Chriftians, is but fmall.—The languages are fo many and fo various, that there is no poffibility of reducing them to any certain number though the chief are the Turkifh, the Grecian, the Arabic, the Chinefe, the Perfian, and the old Indian; in fhort, every country has almoft a diftinct language. Befides the animals we have in Europe, there are lions, leopards, tigers, camels, elephants, rhinocerofes, and many others. The air of this very extenfive divifion of the globe may naturally be fuppofed to be various: Thofe who live near the line are in a manner melted by the exceffive heat of the fun, while the inhabitants of the frigid zone are almoft frozen. Such however, is the wife difpenfation of Providence, that he forms his creatures fuitable to the climate in which he gives them exiftence. The inhabitants of the Frozen Zone could no more endure the heat of the equinoctial line, than beings born in thofe hot climates could live under the cold of the Polar regions. Not only men, but even every animal is clothed fuitably to the climate in which he is to exift; it is obferved, that fuch birds as are peculiar to cold countries are covered with a thick down, which is not the cafe with thofe that are found in warmer countries.

AFRICA

Pᵗ of ASIA

ARABIA
Medina
Aden
Red Sea

Medit
Mediterranean Sea

Abissinia
Ajan
Adel
Magadoxo
Brava
Melinda
Mombaza
Quiloa

EASTERN OCEAN

Natal
Dᵒ of Bourbon
Brumais
Mauritius
MADAGASCAR
I. de Ascen
R. de Natal
Cape of Good Hope
Table B.
Hottentots

BARBARY
SARA of the DESART
NEGROLAND
GUINEA
Benin
Loango
Congo
Angola
Benguela
Matamba
Monomotapa
Sofala

Tropic of Cancer
Canary Is
Cape Verd Is
Equinoctial Line
Tropic of Capricorn

ETHIOPIC OCEAN

OCEAN

AFRICA.

AFRICA is a peninfula joined to Afia, by the Ifthmus of Suez; is fituated between 18° weft, and
50° eaftern longitude, and between 37° north and 35°
fouth latitude. It is bounded by the Mediterranean
Sea, which divides it from Europe, on the north; by
the Ifthmus of Suez, the Red fea, and the Indian Ocean,
on the eaft; by the Southern Ocean on the fouth; and
by the Atlantic Ocean on the weft.—This quarter of
the world is varioufly divided according to different
geographers; the beft arrangement is Egypt, Barbary,
Guinea, Congo, Caffraria, Abyffinia, Nubia, and
Nigritia, with the iflands which furround it. The
greateft part of it is within the Torrid Zone, which
renders the heat almoft infupportable in many places;
yet the coafts in general are very fruitful, the fruits
excellent, and the plants far beyond what could be
reafonably expected. Here are more wild beafts than
in any other part of the world, and particularly the
fea-horfe, whofe teeth are fo large that they fupply
the place of ivory, and by many are preferred to it.
From hence comes the beautifully ftriped zebra, which
is efteemed a prefent worthy the acceptance of the
greateft princes. Crocodiles are not here met with fo
frequently as formerly, but from what caufe is not
eafily to be afcertained. They have likewife oftriches,
camels, various fpecies of monkies, and feveral other
animals not to be met with in Europe.—There are
many deferts, fome of which are of a large extent, and
almoft without water. Such is the loofe texture of their
fands, that when the wind blows ftrong, they will fome-

B 4   times

times bury whole caravans at a time. Nature feems to have formed the camel for the ufe of the natives when they travel over thefe barren fands, fince that animal will travel fifteen days without water. Thefe deferts, however, are not totally deftiftute of inhabitants; for there are wild Arabs and other people, who rove from one part to another, partly in fearch of pafture, and partly to lie in ambufh for the rich caravans that travel from Barbary and Egypt to Negroeland and Abyffinia. There are many high mountains in fome parts, particularly in Abyffinia and Barbary; in which laft country is Mount Atlas, that feparates Barbary from Biledulgerid. The principal river in Africa is the Nile, which runs through very extenfive countries. It has its fource at the foot of a high mountain, in the province of Goyam in Abyffinia; runs from thence into Nubia, and then into Egypt, till it arrives at Cairo; a little below which it divides itfelf in two great branches, which, with the Mediterranean Sea, form the ifland called the Delta, fancifully fo called, from its refembling in fhape the figure of the Greek letter called by that name, $\triangle$. The Niger is another capital river in Africa, which is thought by fome to have its fource near that of the Nile, and to run quite acrofs Africa, till it falls into the Atlantic Ocean by feveral branches, of which Senegal is the chief; but the courfe of the river is not fo well afcertained as that of the Nile. The inhabitants are for the moft part tawny, and in fome parts quite black. There are travellers who accufe fome of thefe people of feeding on human flefh; but the fact is much doubted.

NORTH AMERICA

THE NORTH CONTINENT

Baffins Bay

Esquimaux

Green Land

Arctic Circle

N. North Wales

C. Farwell

Hudsons Bay

NORTH SEA

James Bay

N. South Wales

Labrador

Newfound Land

Nootka Sound

The Lakes

CANADA
Quebec

Boston
Halifax

New York

UNITED STATES

ATLANTIC

Mexico or NEW SPAIN

LOUISIANA

Mississippi R.

Bermudas Is.

OCEAN

California

Florida

GULF OF MEXICO

Tropic of Cancer

WEST

Campechy B.

St. Domingo

INDIES

THE SOUTH SEA

Jamaica

Trinidad

Pt. OF SOUTH AMERICA

AMERICA.

AMERICA, the weſtern continent, frequently de-
nominated the *New World* (*being lately diſcovered*),
is ſituated between 35° and 145° of weſtern longitude.
It is bounded on the lands and ſeas about the Arctic
Pole, on the north; by the Atlantic Ocean, which ſepa-
rates it from the eaſtern continent, on the eaſt; by the
vaſt Southern Ocean on the ſouth; and by the Pacific
Ocean, which divides it from Aſia, on the weſt. It is
divided into North and South America, of the particular diviſions of each of which we ſhall ſpeak hereafter
in their proper places. Chriſtopher Columbus, a na-
tive of Genoa, was the firſt who undertook to extend
the boundaries which ignorance had given to the world.
He ſailed from Spain in 1491, and, after a voyage of
thirty-three days, he landed on one of thoſe iſlands
now called the Bahamas. He afterwards touched on
ſeveral of the iſlands in the ſame cluſter, enquiring
every where for gold, which was the only object of
commerce he thought worth his attention. All directed him to a great iſland, called Bohio, of which they
were laviſh in their praiſes, and principally on account
of its abounding in the precious metal which he ſought
for. By their directions, he fortunately found this
iſland, to which he afterwards gave the name of Hiſpa-
niola. On his return home, he touched on ſeveral
of the iſlands to the ſouthward, and diſcovered the
Caribbees. He was welcomed in Spain with all the
acclamations which the populace are ever ready to
give on ſuch occaſions, and the court received him with
the higheſt marks of reſpect. He afterwards ſailed on

other

other difcoveries to America; but the ungrateful and avaricious Spaniards, not immediately receiving thofe golden advantages they had promifed themfelves from his firft voyages, at laft fuffered him to die neglected and difregarded. The court of Spain, however, were fo juft to his memory, that they buried him magnificently in the cathedral of Seville, and erected a tomb over him, with this infcription : *Columbus has given a new world to the kingdoms of Caftile and Leon.*——The wealth which Columbus brought into Europe tempted many perfons to make equipments at their own expence. In one of thefe expeditions the famous Americus Vefpufius commanded, in the life-time of Columbus, whofe charts he had found means to get into his poffeffion, and by them failed the fame courfe. As he was a man of addrefs and great confidence, and was befides an able feaman and good geographer, he found a way of arrogating to himfelf the firft difcovery of the continent of America, and called it by his own name, which it has ever fince retained; though no one refufes to give that honour to Columbus. It is impoffible here to mention the various particulars of the difcoveries of this continent; fuffice it to fay, that Cortez, in the year 1512, made the Spaniards mafters of Mexico, after having deftroyed upwards of one hundred thoufand of the inhabitants in the moft cruel manner. The conqueft of Peru, &c. by Pizarro and his affociates, was attended with deeds equally atrocious. The principal motive of the Spaniards in fending fo many colonies here was undoubtedly the thirft of gold; and, indeed, they and the Portuguefe are poffeffed of all thofe parts where it is found in the greateft plenty.

SOUTH AMERICA

J. Roeca Sc.

No. 6.

A M E R I C A, continued.

AMERICA is certainly that part of the world which is the best watered, and that not only for the support of life, but for the convenience of trade, and the intercourse of each part with the other. In North America, the great river Missisippi, rising from unknown sources, runs an immense course from north to south, and receives the vast tribute of the Ohio, and other extensive rivers, which are navigable almost to their very sources. Many parts are so interfected with navigable rivers and creeks, that the planters may be justly said to have each an harbour at his own door. South America is supplied by much the two largest rivers in the world, the river Amazons and the Rio de la Plata. The first rising in Peru, not far from the South Sea, passes from west to east, almost quite through the continent of South America, navigable all the way, and receiving into its bosom a prodigious number of other rivers, all navigable, and so considerable, that Monf. de la Condamine found it almost impossible to determine which was the main channel. The Rio de la Plata, rising in the heart of the country, shapes its course to the south-east, and pours such an immense flood into the sea, that it makes it taste fresh a great many leagues from the shore; to say nothing of the Oroonoque, which might rank the foremost among any but the American rivers. The Indians of America are tall, and straight in their limbs, beyond the proportion of most nations; but their bodies, though strong, are not fitted to endure so much labour as the Europeans. Their heads are rendered flattish, by art; their fea-

tures

tures are regular, but their countenances fierce, and their hair long, black, and lank. There are no people among whom the laws of hospitality are more sacred, or executed with more generosity and good will. Their houses and provisions are not enough to oblige a strange guest, and to those of their own nation they are likewise very humane and beneficent, but to the enemies of his country, or those who have privately offended him, the American Indian is implacable. He conceals his sentiments, he appears reconciled, until, by some treachery or surprise, he has an opportunity of executing a horrible revenge. No length of time is sufficient to allay his resentment, no distance great enough to protect the object; he crosses the steepest mountains, he pierces almost impenetrable forests, and traverses the most hideous bogs and desarts, for several hundred miles, bearing the inclemency of the seasons, the fatigue of the expedition, the extremes of hunger and thirst, with patience and chearfulness, in hopes of surprising his enemy, on whom he exercises the most shocking barbarities. Liberty, in its fullest extent, is their darling passion : To this they sacrifice every thing, and this is what makes a life of uncertainty and want supportable to them : Their education is directed in such a manner as to cherish this to the utmost extent. Almost their sole occupation is war, and he is little regarded in their councils who has not given some proof of his valour. The chief qualities of an Indian warrior are vigilance and attention, to give and to avoid a surprise; and patience and strength, to endure the almost intolerable fatigues and hardships which constantly attend it.

63   67   71   75   79

A Scale of Miles 60 to a Deg.

BRITAIN
and
IRELAND

J.T. Scott sculp. Philad?

Faro I.

Mainland

Just I.
Fetlar I.
Shetland I?
Brassa Sound

Sky I. Wrath

Orkney I.
Dungsboy H?

Kinard's H?

Western
Islands

ATLANTIC

Ila I.

North C.
I. of Arran

GERMAN

Red Castle

SCOTLAND

Flamberough H.
Spurn H?

OCEAN

IRELAND

I. Man

Dingle
C. Clear

Dublin

ENGLAND

WALES

St. GEORGE'S CHANNEL

Bristol Chan.

Land's End
Scilly Is.

London

Dover

OCEAN

Lizard P.
ENGLISH CHANNEL
Guernsey I.
Jersey I.
Great Har

FRANCE

Long. E. from Philad.

63   67   71   75   79

GREAT BRITAIN AND IRELAND.

GREAT BRITAIN is divided into South and North Britain, or into the kingdoms of England and Scotland —ENGLAND is of a triangular form, bounded on the north by Scotland ; on the eaſt, by the German Sea ; on the ſouth, by the Engliſh Channel, which divides it from France ; and on the weſt, by St. George's, or the Iriſh Channel. Situated between 2° eaſt, and 6° 20 weſt longitude; and between 50° and 56ᶜ north latitude. The principal rivers in England are the Thames, the Medway, the Severn, and the Trent. This iſland formerly had very extenſive woods and foreſt ; but at preſent thoſe of the New Foreſt, Dean, Sherwood, and Windſor, are the principal. The air is not ſo cold in winter, nor ſo hot in ſummer, as in countries on the continent which lie under the ſame degree of latitude ; but then it is not ſo pure ; nor have we at any ſeaſon of the year that ſettled weather which they enjoy. On the other hand, on the continent, while the heat of the ſun in one ſeaſon of the year, and the intenſe cold of the other, ſeem to deſtroy all vegetation, we enjoy a perpetual verdure ; and, excepting a very few places, the air is generally eſteemed healthful, from many inſtances of longevity. The ſoil, fruits animals, and produce of this country, are well known.

SCOTLAND is ſituated between 1° and 6° weſtern longitude, and between 54° and 59° of north latitude. It is bounded by the Caledonian Ocean on the north ; by the German Sea on the eaſt ; by the river Tweed, the Tiviot Hill, and the river Eſk, which divides it from England,

GREAT BRITAIN AND IRELAND.

England, on the fouth; and the Irifh Sea and the Atlantic Ocean, on the weft. The air of this country is very cold, owing to its northern fituation, and its mountainous furface. The mountains, or highlands, are covered with almoft perpetual fnows; but in the vallies, and towards the fouth, the air is much warmer. The foil of Scotland is in general very barren, though there are fome fruitful vallies; and Lothian and Fife are faid to be very defirable countries. In the highlands, however, oats is almoft the only grain, of which they make both bread and beer.

IRELAND is fituated between 5° and 10° weftern longitude, and between 51° and 56° northern latitude. It is bounded on the north, weft, and fouth, by the Atlantic Ocean, and by St. George's Channel, which divides it from England on the eaft. The air of Ireland is moift and foggy, like that of England, though fnow is feldom feen here of more than three days continuance. The foil is in many places very fruitful, and fit to be employed under pafturage, meadow, or tillage. It produces hemp and flax, of which a confiderable quantity is raifed here, efpecially in the northern parts of the kingdom. Their breed of cattle is very confiderable, and this formerly was the greateft natural wealth of the inhabitants; indeed, it ftill continues to make a material article in their exports. Every one knows to what perfection they have carried the linen manufacture, which may be confidered as their ftaple article.

ENGLISH Count.
1. Northumberland
2. Cumberland
3. Durham
4. Westmorland
5. York
6. Lancaster
7. Lincoln
8. Nottingham
9. Derbie
10. Chester
11. Stafford
12. Leicester
13. Rutland
14. Cambridge
15. Huntingdon
16. Northampton
17. Warwick
18. Shrop
19. Hertford
20. Worcester
21. Glocester
22. Oxford
23. Bucks
24. Bedford
25. Hartford
26. Essex
27. Suffolk
28. Norfolk
29. Kent
30. Surry
31. Middlesex
32. Sussex
33. Southampton
34. Berks
35. Wilts
36. Dorset
37. Somerset
38. Monmouth
39. Devon
40. Cornwall

ENGLAND
and
WALES

J.T. Scott sculp. Philad.

Welsh Coun.
a. Anglesey
b. Caernarien
c. Denbigh
d. Flint
e. Merioneth
f. Montgomery
g. Cardigan
h. Radnor
i. Brecknock
k. Glamorgan
l. Carmarthen
m. Pembroke

NORTH

SCOTLAND

Edinburgh

Newcastle

Durham

Whitby

Scarbro

Richmond

York

Carlisle

IRISH

SEA

Pontefract

Sheffield

Liverpool

Chester

Lincoln

Nottingham

Man

Yarmouth

Norwich

Ely

Ipswich

Shrewsbury

Leicester

Stafford

Oxford

Glocester

London

Reading

Salisbury

Winchester

Canterbury

Chichester

Bristol Ch.

Exeter

Fowey

Penzance

Lizard Pt.

Isle of Wight

S.[t] or Dover

ENGLISH CHANNEL

FRANCE

ENGLAND AND WALES.

WE have already mentioned the boundaries, situation, &c. of this kingdom, we shall now therefore proceed to speak of the genius and temper of the inhabitants.—Foreigners usually ascribe to the English a very odd medley of virtues and vices, of excellencies and defects. It has been said that they are active, courageous, thoughtful, and devout; lovers of the liberal arts, and as capable of reaching the summit of science as any people in the world; that the more strangers were acquainted with the English, the more they would love and esteem them. On the other hand, it is asserted they are passionate, melancholy, fickle, and unsteady.—The Welch, in general, are a brave and faithful people : They love one another, particularly when in foreign countries, and they are kind to strangers in their own, though they are exceedingly hot and choleric. Wales was incorporated with England, by act of parliament, in 1536, in the reign of Henry VIII.—England abounds in large and fine rivers, which afford great plenty of excellent fish, and serve abundantly the uses of navigation and commerce. It is diversified, in the most agreeable manner, with arable land, meadows, and woods, and here and there with rising hills; and its forests agreeably serve for the pleasure of various prospects, and the delights of hunting. This country in general is exceeded by none for its variety of roots and herbs, and plenty is so constant, that a famine has not been known here for ages. Our wool is famous throughout the world, and the finest and most serviceable cloth is made of it. We have plenty of timber

ber and other materials for building, and our oak is perhaps no where to be equalled. Though there is scarce any fruit natural to our soil, yet almoſt all the fruits of Europe, as well as thoſe of the Weſt Indies, have been introduced here. The minerals dug out of the earth render ſome of the moſt barren parts of the country as valuable as thoſe whoſe ſoil is moſt fruitful; a prodigious quantity of coal ſupplies the country with fuel, enables them to ſeparate metals, and to work them up into an infinite variety of forms, ſo as to fur-niſh a vaſt number of implements and conveniences of life, not only for ourſelves, but our neighbours. We have mines of iron, copper, tin, and lead, and of the two laſt, vaſt quantities are exported. England has not only the advantage of an extenſive commerce, but of manufacturing the goods on which commerce is founded. The commodities produced by the labour of the induſtrious, from things originally of a ſmall price, receiving value from the hands of the workman, are carried to the utmoſt limits of the world, and ſold at a great price. The prodigious number of trading towns, almoſt every one of which has a manufacture peculiar to itſelf, naturally cauſes a great inland trade, a cir-culation of ſpecie throughout the whole country, and ſuch a reciprocal connection between the intereſts of the capital and the moſt diſtant towns, as is greatly for the advantage of the whole. From hence ſmall villages have, in proceſs of time, become populous and flouriſhing cities. Add to theſe advantages, that the Engliſh enjoy the fineſt fiſheries in all the world.

SCOTLAND

Shetland I.

Scale of Miles 60 to a Deg.

J.T. Scott sculp. Philada.

No. 9.

SCOTLAND.

THE principal rivers in Scotland are the Tweed, Clyde, Tay, and Spay, all navigable, besides many lakes, of which Lomund and Rofs are the moft remarkable. Scotland is limited to fixteen Peers, and forty-five Commoners, to fit in the Britifh Parliament at Weftminfter, according to the Union-Act, which fubjects both kingdoms to the fame government. They have many forts of fruit in Scotland, and good roots both for food and phyfic. The Highlands afford good timber; they have coal in many parts of the country, and in the north, firewood, turf, peat, heath, broom, and furze, enough for fuel. They have large flocks of fheep, and herds of black cattle, much fmaller than thofe of England. Numbers of thefe cattle are annually drove into England in a lean condition, and fatted in our meadows and marfhes. Glafgow is the moft confiderable port in the kingdom for foreign traffic, particularly to America and Guinea. They trade moftly in herrings, coals, butter, eggs, tallow, &c. but the greateft advantages Scotland can boaft of are its fifheries: Thefe might prove a mine of infinite wealth to the whole ifland, as they have been to the Dutch, and would add more to our ftrength and fuperiority at fea, than all our foreign traffic; for here we might breed many thoufands of hardy feamen that would always be at hand to man our fleets, when the reft are abfent upon diftant voyages. As the natives can cure the fifh cheaper and fooner than the Dutch, and may be a month fooner at market, confidering how far the Dutch have to fail backwards and forwards, and what

numbers

SCOTLAND.

numbers of doggers and tenders they are obliged to employ, the Britiſh Nation ſeems to be infatuated, to have ſo long neglected to promote and eſtabliſh the herring fiſhery, in which all our poor, had we ten times more, might be employed on ſhore, in making and mending nets, ſails, cordage, &c.—The iſlands of Scotland may be divided into three claſſes : The Hebrides, or Weſtern Iſlands, which anciently went under the name of *Hebrides* : The iſles of Orkney, or Orcades, in the Caledonian Ocean, on the north of Scotland ; and the iſles of Shetland, ſtill farther north-eaſt.—The weſtern iſlands are very numerous, and ſome of them large, particularly that of Skye, ſeparated from the main land by a very narrow channel. The moſt weſterly of theſe iſlands is that of St. Kilda, which is a rock riſing almoſt perpendicular in the ſea, and is nearly inacceſſible. It is about five miles in circumference, and has a ſtaple of earth ſufficient to produce barley and oats. The inhabitants are about 300 proteſtants ; their houſes are of ſtone, and they lie in little cabins in the walls upon ſtraw.—The Orkney iſlands are divided from the continent by Penthland Frith, a ſea which is remarkable for its ſwift and contrary tides, which make it a very dangerous paſſage for ſtrangers. There are violent whirlpools that whirl about both ſhips and boats till they founder, and are moſt dangerous in a calm.—The iſlands of Shetland are reckoned forty-ſix in number, the largeſt of which is called Mainland. The ſeas of this, like the reſt, are very tempeſtuous and dangerous.

IRELAND
J.T. Scott sculp. Philad.a
Scale of Miles 60 to a Deg.
Donnegall Bay
Sligo
Mayo
CONNAUGHT
Gallway
Tyrone
Down
Cavan
Meath
Dublin
LEINSTER
Queens
Wicklow
Wexford
Kilkenny
Tipperary
Limerick
MUNSTER
Cork
Kerry
Waterford
Clare
Dreghedah
Carlingford
Strangford
Belfast
Antrim
Colrain
Giants Causeway
Killala
Roscommon
Longford
Kings
Kildare
Carlow
Cashel
Kinsale
Bantry
Ross
Dingle
Arklow
Wexford
Mizen H.
Lon. E. from Philad.a
ATLANTIC OCEAN
IRISH SEA

IRELAND.

THE Irish in general are a strong-bodied people, nimble, and active; bold, haughty, intrepid, and violent in all their affections. They are reproached for want of genius, and some have gone so far as to call them a nation of blunderers; but these aspersions are unjust, since Ireland has produced men of as great learning, and of as elevated a genius, as any nation in Europe can boast of. Their bravery and military skill cannot be disputed, any more than those of their neighbours the Scotch.—Since Ireland became subject to the crown of England, the constitution of the government there has varied but little from that of the mother country. The kings of England have always sent viceroys thither to administer the public affairs in their name, and by their authority. They have likewise their Houses of Lords and Commons, as we have. The established religion of Ireland is the same as in England; but not near a fourth part of the Inhabitants are members of the church of England: Besides the papists, who are at least three to one, the dissenters of all persuasions are very numerous, especially about Londonderry, and in the north.—The discouragements laid on Ireland by the act of navigation, and other laws made in England, are so many, that it cannot be expected that this country should flourish so much in trade, as its natural situation, its rivers, bays, and harbours, commodious for navigation, would seem to promise; nor is Ireland so well peopled as formerly, owing principally to the avariciousness of the landholders, who have extravagantly raised their rents.

The

IRELAND.

The fame thing is done in Scotland; and on this account emigrations are daily making from both thofe countries. In Ireland, fome thoufands of acres are now unoccupied, and many more are foon likely to become fo, unlefs fome proper means are thought of to induce the natives to ftay in their own country—The principal rivers in Ireland are the Barrow, the Nore, the Suir, and the Boyne; but the Shannon is the nobleft and largeft of them all. The banks of this river are adorned with feveral towns of confequence, befides pleafant feats, and villages innumerable. It is remarkable alfo for many overflowings of its waters, called loughs, in which are many pleafant and profitable iflands; but with all the advantages and beauties of this river, it has one great defect, which is a ridge of rocks fouth of Killaloe, fpreading quite acrofs it : Thefe caufe a cataract or waterfal, and ftop all navigation further up, otherwife, this river being fo wide and deep, might eafily be made navigable almoft to its fource. Here are likewife many lakes; and among thefe is Lough-Larne, in the county of Kerry, which is about fix Englifh miles in length, and near half as much broad at a medium. It is interfperfed with a variety of beautiful iflands, many of them rich in herbage, and well inhabited. Eagles and ofpreys are here in great number, and groves of the Arbutus, which moft part of the year bears a fcarlet fruit like the ftrawberry. In fhort, the beauties of this lake are not be defcribed, nor feen without raptures.

The UNITED PROVINCES

GERMANY

GRONINGEN

FRIESLAND

OVERYSSEL

GELDERLAND

UTRECHT

ZUYDER ZEE

HOLLAND

FLANDERS

GERMAN OCEAN

Embden

Ems

Groeningen

Dam

Leuwarden

Harlingen

Snuck

Staeven

Haerlem

Texel I.

Vliland I.

Schelling I.

Inveland I.

Medenblick

Pellen

N.

Zuyden

Deventer

Bentham

Rhine R.

Meuse R.

Scale of Miles 60 to a Deg.

Lon. E. from Philadª.

Engd. by T. Scott sculp. Philadª.

THE UNITED PROVINCES.

THE United Netherlands are bounded on the east by Upper Germany, on the west and north by part of the German Ocean, and on the south by Flanders. They confist of seven provinces, Holland, Zealand, Utrecht, Guelderland, Overyssel, Groningen, and Friesland. In the provinces of Holland is Amsterdam, one of the richest and noblest trading cities in the world. Harlem is a large and noble city, in which there is a great manufactory of fine hollands, flowered silks, and fine lace. Leyden, next to Amsterdam, is the finest city in Holland; and has always been famous for its university. Delft is a pleasant city : Here is a great arfenal, out of which 100,000 men may be armed. The Hague confifts chiefly of outlets and gardens : The ftates-general of the United Provinces affemble here, and this place is the refort of moft foreign ambassadors and minifters.—The air of this country is generally thick and moift, on account of the frequent fogs which arife from the many lakes and canals with which it abounds; and to this are attributed the frequent complaints of agues, to which the inhabitants are fubject. As to the foil, it is naturally wet and fenny, the country lying very low ; but the induftry of the inhabitants has made it very fit both for pafture and tillage. Though the commodities of this country, proceeding from its own growth, may, ftrictly fpeaking, be reckoned only butter and cheefe, yet, on account of the many ufeful manufactures which this people encourage at home, the materials for which are brought from other nations, and the amazing trade

C 3   which

which they manage abroad in moſt parts of the known world, we may reckon it a public warehouſe of the richeſt and beſt commodities of all nations. The natives are reckoned not polite either in thought or behaviour, eſpecially the latter, yet they are allowed to be poſſeſſed of a wonderful ſhare of induſtry, with which they ſeem to be univerſally inſpired, perſons of all ages, ſexes and ſtations, being ſome way or other uſefully employed. Every claſs of men are extremely frugal, every man ſpending leſs than his income, be that what it wil. All appetites and paſſions run cooler and lower here than in other countries, avarice excepted; quarrels are very rare, revenge ſeldom heard of, and jealouſy ſcarce ever known. Their tempers are not airy enough for joy, nor warm enough for love: This indeed is ſometimes talked of among their young fellows as a thing they have heard of, but never felt. It is very rare for any of them to be in love, nor do the women ſeem to care whether they are or not.—The United Provinces form, as it were, ſeveral commonwealths, each province being a diſtinct ſtate, with an independent power within itſelf to judge of all cauſes, of what kind ſoever, and to inflict even capital puniſhments; but all, joined together, make up one republic, the moſt conſiderable in the world. They are governed by the aſſembly of the ſtates general, conſiſting of ſeven voices, each province having one. Matters are not determined in this aſſembly by a plurality of voices; for all the provinces muſt come to an unanimous conſent before any thing can be done.

The NETHER=LANDS

GERMANY

FRANCE

GERMAN OCEAN

BRABANT

D. BRABANT

S. BRABANT

LIEGE

BISHOP.

LUXEMBURG

FLANDERS

FRENCH FL.

ARTOIS

Hainault

Antwerp

Namur

Luxemburg

Arlon

Bouillon

Sedan

Charleville

Charlemont

Cambray

Philat?

Abbeville

Calais

Dunkirk

Scale of Miles of 60 to a Deg.

I. Scott sculp.

Lon. E. from Philad?

THE NETHERLANDS.

THE Netherlands are bounded by the United Provinces on the north; by Germany on the east; by Lorrain, Champagne, and Picardy, in France, on the south; and by another part of Picardy, and the English Sea on the west.—In the time of Charles the Fifth, this country and the seven United Provinces were added to the empire of Germany, under the title of the Circle of Burgundy, the whole consisting of seventeen provinces. After his death, they descended to his son, Philip the Second, king of Spain; but, on his endeavouring to deprive the natives of their liberties and privileges, they revolted; and, after several bloody wars, he was at last obliged to part with seven of the provinces, and, by the peace of Westphalia, to declare them a free people. The division may now more properly be called, 1. The ten provinces of the Austrian and French Netherlands; and, 2. The seven provinces of the United Netherlands, already described.—The air of the Austrian and French Netherlands is generally much better than that of the United Provinces, except on the coast of Flanders and Brabant, where it is very unhealthy. Their winters are usually more severe than ours; but then they have more constant weather both winter and summer, in the inland part of the country, than we enjoy. Their soil is in some parts a deep rich mould, in others a barren sand; in the former are large corn-fields, pasture grounds, and plenty of forest and fruit trees. Their principal manufactures consist of fine lawns, cambric, lace, and tapestry, with which they maintain a very advantageous traffic, especially

with

with England, from whom it is computed they receive a balance of half a million annually in time of peace. There are no very confiderable mountains in this country : Flanders has not a fingle hill in it : Brabant and, the reft of the provinces confift of little hills and valles, woods, inclofed grounds, and champaign fields : The forefts of Ardenne and Soignies are the moft confiderable woods. Their principal rivers are the Maefe and the Scheldt, befides many extenfive canals.—The genius and temper of thefe people are like thofe of the French, in thofe parts which lie near France, but in Dutch Flanders or Brabant, they are mere Dutchmen. The head of the houfe of Auftria, (who is ufually the Emperor of Germany) is fovereign of thefe provinces and in him or his viceroy, and the convention of the eftates of the refpective provinces, is the legiflative power of each lodged. Here new laws are enacted, and by their affent alone is money levied : The whole affembly muft be unanimous in paffing of an act. The affembly or parliament of each province confifts, 1. Of the bifhops, abbots, and dignified clergy; 2. The nobility and gentry, and 3. The deputies or reprefentatives of the chief towns. Thefe meet at Brufiels, except thofe of Luxembourgh and Guilders, who, by their ancient privileges, cannot be fummoned out of their refpective provinces, any more than the ftates of Brabant. Neither do the ftates of the feveral provinces, which meet at Brufiels, affemble in one houfe, but each of them apart, and make diftinct laws for their refpective countries. Befides the regent or governor general, every province has its peculiar governor, fubject to the regent; and in every province are courts of juftice, eftablifhed for the trial of civil caufes.

No. 13.

FRANCE.

THIS republic is fituated between 5° weft and 8° eaft lo. gitude, and between 42° and 52° of north latitude. It is bounded by the Englifh channel and the United Provinces on the north; by Germany, Switzerland, and Italy, on the eaft; by the Mediterranean and Pyrenean mountains, on the fouth; and by the Bay of Bifcay, on the weft.—The principal mountains in this republic are the Alps, which divide France from Italy; the Pyrenees, which feparate it from Spain; and the Vague, Mount Jura, and the Cevennes, of lefs note.—The Rhone, the Saone, the Garonne, the Charante, the Loire, the Seine, and the Rhine, are the principal rivers that water this fpacious country.—The air of France is temperate, but much warmer than that of England, particularly in the fouthern parts, where, efpecially about Montpelier, it is fo very healthy, that no part of Europe is faid to be equal to it. However, in fome parts, the fun is fo very powerful, at particular feafons, as to admit of no appearance of verdure; but for this they are in fome meafure repaid by excellent wine, oil, and fruits of various kinds, which cannot be procured in fuch perfection elfewhere. Though they have nearly the fame animals as England, yet their beafts of burden are not fo good; and their manufactures, though they have raifed them to fuch a pitch as to equal, and in fome inftances to excel, in appearance, thofe of England, whofe rivals they are in trade, yet they are not finifhed in fo mafterly a manner. As to their trade, there is hardly any part of the globe which their merchantmen do not vifit; their fifheries alfo are

C 5   very

FRANCE.

very confiderable. The conftitution of France, was lately an abfolute government; and though they had parliaments, they were merely nominal, having but little power. It is at prefent a republic.---The executive power is lodged in five directors.---The legiflative in two houfes---one a Council of Ancients, of 250 members; the other called the Council of 500, from the number of members of which it is compofed. The revenues are computed at about fifteen millions fterling. The ftature of the French people is rather low; and, though they are not fo ftout and robuft as the inhabitants of the northern nations, they are neverthelefs well made, and are remarkably nimble and active. They are in general ftrangers to melancholy, and hence bear misfortunes with great fortitude and refignation. Their heroifm during their revolution, efpecially that of their army of Italy under Buonaparte, has equalled, perhaps exceeded that of ancient Rome, when at its utmoft glory.---The city of Paris is of itfelf a curiofity, being one of the largeft and moft beautiful cities in Europe. It is faid to confift of 50,000 houfes, of which 500 are very large, and are called *Hotels*. The univerfity of Paris is the moft ancient in Europe, it having been founded by Charlemagne in 790: It is compofed of three colleges, of which that for divinity is called the Sorbonne. There are likewife feveral famous academies, among which are thofe of infcriptions and belles lettres; of fciences, painting, fculpture, &c.

SPAIN and PORTUGAL

A. Ellicott sculp.

FRANCE

BAY of BISCAY

ATLANTIC

OCEAN

MEDITERRANEAN SEA

Scale of Miles 60 to a D.

Lon. E. from Philad.

AFRICA

C. Ortegal
C. Finisterre
Galicia
Leon
Oviedo
Asturias
Biscay
Bilboa
Navarre
St. Sebastian
Pampeluna
Catalonia
Barcelona
Tortosa
Tarragona
Aragon
Old Castile
Valladolid
Burgos
Zamora
Salamanca
Madrid
New Castile
Valencia
Valencia
Cuença
Murcia
Carthagena
Granada
Cordova
Seville
Cadiz
Gibraltar
C. Spartel
Andalusia
Malaga
Alboran I.
Tarifa
PORTUGAL
Lisbon
Oporto
Coimbra
C. Roca
C. St. Vincent
Lagos
Majorca I.
Minorca I.
Port Mahon
Ivica I.

36

40

20

25

21

23

22

SPAIN AND PORTUGAL.

SPAIN is fituated between 10° weft and 3° eaft longitude, between 36° and 44° north latitude. It is bounded on the weft by Portugal and the Atlantic Ocean; by the Mediterranean on the eaft; by the Bay of Bifcay, and the Pyrenean Hills on the north; and by the Straits of Gibraltar, on the fouth.—Portugal lies between 7° and 10° weft longitude, and between 37° and 42° north latitude. It is bounded by part of Spain on the north and eaft, and by the Atlantic Ocean on the fouth and weft.—The principal mountains in Spain are the Pyrenees, which divide that kingdom from France, and extend 200 miles from the Bay of Bifcay to the Mediterranean Sea. Portugal is no lefs mountainous than Spain, and thefe mountains are for the moft part barren rocks.—The moft remarkable rivers in Spain are the Douro, the Guadiana, which runs four leagues under ground, the Guadalquiver, the Ebro, and the Tajo. The Tagus is the chief river of Portugal.—The air of Spain is generally dry, pure, and ferene, except about the equinoxes, when their rains ufually fall. In the fummer months they are fubject to great heats, in the fouthern parts; though on the mountains, and near the coaft, they are refrefhed with cool breezes: It is very cold in winter on the mountains in the north and northeaft. Though there are fome fandy barren defarts in the fouth, yet their vallies in general are very fruitful, and their mountains are covered with trees and herbage to the very top of them. They abound in variety of rich wines, oils, and fruits. Befides filks, fine wool, flax and cotton,

which

SPAIN AND PORTUGAL.

which Spain produces in abundance, there are mines of quickfilver, fteel, copper, lead, and alum. The fteel of Toledo and Bilboa is efteemed the beft in Europe. Portugal, being a hot country, wants neither wine nor oil; but, on account of its many hills and mountains, corn is very fcarce, with which it is fupplied from other countries.—Spain is governed by an abfolute monarch, and none but the Roman catholic religion is tolerated in that country.—The Spaniards are men of wit, and of an elevated genius, but very little improved by ftudy or converfation : They are admired for their fecrecy, conftancy, and patience in adverfity : They are flow in determining, but ufually conclude judicioufly at laft : True to their word, great enemies to lying, and extremely temperate in eating and drinking. On the other hand, they are proud, lazy, luftful, entirely neglecting manufactures and hufbandry.—The Portuguefe were once a valiant people, and famous, not only for their fkill in navigation, but for their firft difcoveries in Africa and America. At prefent, Portugal is little better than a kingdom of priefts, monks, and nuns, who entirely devour the fubftance of the country, without being in a condition of affording the ftate the leaft fervice in its moft preffing exigencies. The principal employment of the Portuguefe is trade, and their merchants have all the vices which too often attend it. As to learning, that is now on the decline, and their academics and fchools are gone to decay. Ever fince the revolution in 1640, Portugal has continued an independent kingdom from Spain, fubject only to their own kings, whofe government is monarchical and the crown hereditary.

45

ITALY

Scale of Miles Geloa Hes.

J.T.Scott sculp. Philad?

GERMANY

Carniola

Savoy

VENICE

TURKY IN EUROPE

Croatia

FRANCE

Milan

Dalmatia

GULF OF VENICE

Rome

Spoleto

MED

Corsica
la Yasse
St. Bonifacio

NAPLES

Corfu I.

Algeri

ITER

Naples

Oristagni

St. Pietro I.
Antische I.
Caglian
C. Tavelare
Cherby
Rocks

Palermo

Lipari I.

Regio

SICILY

Messina

RANEAN SEA

Terra Nova

Syracuse

Biona
Tunis

Benn

C. Passar

I. de Geze

Malta

AFRICA

Lon. E. from Phi A

ITALY.

ITALY is fituated between 7° and 19° of eaftern
longitude, and between 38° and 47° of northern
latitude. It is bounded by Switzerland and the Alps,
which divide it from Germany, on the north; by another part of Germany, and the Gulf of Venice, on the
eaft; by the Mediterranean, on the fouth; and by the
fame fea, the Alps, and the river Var, which divide it
from France, on the weft.—The principal mountains
are the Alps, on the north and weft; the Appenine,
which runs the whole length of Italy; and Vefuvius, a
remarkable volcano, near Naples—It is watered by the
Adige, which has its fource in the Alps, and empties
itfelf into the Adriatic Sea; the Po, the Arno, and the
Tiber.—Italy is very uneven, on account of the Swifs
mountains and the Alps; but it has plenty of wine,
fruit and oil. It produces a great deal of filk, not only
fufficient for their own manufactories, but for the fupply of other nations. Though there is no great plenty
of corn, yet there is generally enough for the inhabitants; and, in time of fcarcity, they are moftly fupplied
with it from England and other places. The air is
generally very pure, mild, and healthful, except in the
Campagnia di Roma, where, during the fummer feafon,
it is fo peftilential, that few or no people remain in it
that time.—The natives of Italy, once the triumphant
lords and conquerors of the world, are now lefs given
to the arts of war and military exploits, than moft
other nations of Europe: They are, however, witty
and fprightly, famous for vocal and inftrumental mufic,
as well as for painting and fculpture; but extremely

jealous

jealous and revengeful : To accomplish their ends, they spare no expence or pains, and have often recourse to treachery, to destroy those whom they deem their enemies; and hence it is that Italy is charged with being guilty of more murders than any other European country. To the commission of these crimes two things very much contribute : First, the smallness of its states, which makes it very easy to fly from one to another; and, secondly, the conveniency of sanctuaries, the hands of justice not being able to take hold of any murderer who can get into a church, without going through so many formalities as will give the murderer time enough to escape.—Italy is a beautiful country, and with some reason called the garden of Europe : It is the delight and admiration of travellers; its opulent and magnificent cities, stately palaces, churches, monasteries, convents, treasures, and rarities, are surprising, and furnish the curious with more antiquities in sculpture, medals, and other curiosities, than any country besides.—The venetian territories are as fruitful as any in Italy, abounding with vineyards and plantations of mulberries. The road between Verona and Padua is planted so thick with mulberry-trees, that they not only furnish food for vast numbers of silkworms with their leaves, and feed the swine and poultry with their fruit, but serve as so many staves for the vines, which hang all along like garlands from tree to tree. The church of St. Peter at Rome is considered as one of the most beautiful buildings ever seen : St. Paul's in London was taken from that model; but that of St. Peter's is considerably larger, and better adorned with statues and paintings.

SWITZERLAND
with its
Allies
M. J. Escott sculp.

GERMANY

League often Jurisdictions

Appenzel

al

Rakeinburg

Albert Lake

of the Haute

League of

Constance

GRISONS

Glaris

Sabelline

STATES

Lucern

Zurich

CANTON of BERN

Gothard M.

Sign Rhene

ITALY

Como

Lucano

Bern

Thun

Brients

Cau.

Fribourg

Villeneux

THE VALAIS

Basile

Bishop of

Bastil

Zurich

Montbeliard

SAVOY

FRA

Geneva

Lausanne

Leon.E. from Philadt.

SWITZERLAND AND ITS ALLIES.

SWITZERLAND is fituated between 6° and 11° of eaftern longitude, and between 45° and 48° of nor . thern latitude. It is bounded by Alface and Swabia in Germany, on the north; by the Lake of Conftance, Tyrol, and Trent, on the eaft; by Italy, on the fouth; and by France on the weft.—The firft of the cantons is Zurich, the capital of which is fituated on a lake of the fame name, and is the richeft and moft populous city in Switzerland, being famous for its manufactures of crapes, and its learned academy : But the largeft and moft powerful canton is Bern, which is able to raife 60,000 men in twenty-four hours. It is divided into different countries; the firft of which, and the largeft, is called the German Country : and another the Roman Country, or the country of Vaud. There are feveral fmall territories, called the Swifs Subjects, which indeed were admitted by the thirteen cantons into their covenant, not as confederates or allies, but as mere fubjects; the firft of which is the town of Baden, with its territory, which has its name from the hot baths wherewith Nature has ftored it. It is famous on account of being the place of the general meeting of the cantons and their allies. There are other territories and governments about the Swifs, called the Swifs Allies, who have made each a feparate alliance with the cantons, and at different times. The principal of thefe are the republics of Grifons, Vallois, and Geneva, which laft is the moft confiderable. The capital, Geneva, is a large, fine, rich, and populous city, fituate on the lake of that name, which is the largeft in Europe,

SWITZERLAND AND ITS ALLIES.

rope.—Switzerland abounds with high mountains, and
some of them are covered with ice and snow all the
year round; others abound with trees and pasture,
where the peasants drive their cattle to feed, as it were,
above the clouds. In the Alps the difference of seasons
in one and the same climate is very remarkable; for
travellers may, in one day, meet with winter on the
tops of the mountains, the spring on the lower part of
them, with pleasant green pastures, and hay-time and
harvest at the foot of the mountains and in the vallies.
The most remarkable rivers in Switzerland are the
Rhine, the Rhone, and the Aar.—The Swiss are plain
but honest people, true and faithful to their word ;
courageous, strong, and excellent soldiers. As to their
government, they have no prince to preside in their
councils of state : Each canton, and ally of the canton,
is governed by its own magistrate. In some, the government is in the hands of but a few, and in others it
is in the hands of the people. In matters of great im-
portance, not only the cantons, but also the Swiss allies, are convened together, either at Baden or Aran.
In time of need they can raise 200,000 men in a few
hours; for every Swiss is a soldier for his country, and
is enlisted as such when fourteen years of age. When
a signal of danger is given by a fire on the neighbouring hills, he must go immediately to his place of ren-
dezvous, and carry with him four pounds of bullets,
two pounds of powder, and provision for eight days.
—Switzerland produces cattle, fish, wine, milk, butter,
and cheese. Their mountains being covered with snow
great part of the year, and their lakes and rivers frozen, the air is very cold in winter.

GERMANY
divided into
CIRCLES
I.T.Scott sculp.

NORTH

SEA

BALTIC SEA

Bornholm I.

Rugen I.

Danzick

Elbe R.

United Provinces

WESTPHALIA

LOWER SAXONY

UPPER SAXONY

Hannover

Berlin

Lusatia

Leipsic

Dresden

SILESIA

Breslau

POLAND

UPPER & LOWER RHINE

Heneberg

Prague

FRANCO NIA

BOHEMIA

Nuremberg

MORAVIA

Danube R.

HUNGA RY

FRANCE

SWABIA

Rothenberg

Constance L.

BAVARIA

Vienna

Switzer land

Grisons

Tirol

Trent

AUSTRIA

Geneva

Triest

ITALY

TURKY in EUROPE

GERMANY.

GERMANY is situated between 5° and 19° of eastern longitude, and between 45° and 55° of north latitude. It is bounded by the German Sea, Denmark, and the Baltic, on the north; by Poland, Bohemia, and Hungary, on the east; by the Alps, and Switzerland, on the south; and by the territories of France and the Netherlands, on the west.—The principal rivers in Germany are the Danube, which flows from west to east, and falls into the Euxine Sea; the Rhine, the Maine, the Weser, the Elbe, and the Oder. —The air of this country differs considerably according to the situation of the various parts of this extensive continent. It is generally very cold towards the north; but in the southern provinces it is nearly of the same temperature with those places in France which lie under the same parallels; and the soil, like the air, must consequently be very different. In the southern circles, and in the middle part of the continent, there is hardly any country in the world that excels them for plenty of fruits, corn and wine; but towards the north, the soil is not near so fruitful, especially in wine; grapes never coming to full perfection there. On the whole, the country is tolerably pleasant, abounding with all the necessaries of life.—The German manufactures of steel, iron, brass, &c. which they sell extremely cheap, were once said to excel all others in Europe. They are famous for clock-work, guns, and locks of all kinds — As to the manners of these people, they are grave and honest, and generally very fair in their dealings. In either arts or war they are equally excellent, have an

D   extensive

GERMANY.

extensive genius for mechanical learning, and are famous for some singular inventions, particularly that of the fatal instrument the gun.—The inhabitants of Vienna are much given to feasting and carousing, and in general live very luxuriously. When the branches of the Danube are frozen over, and the ground covered with snow, the ladies take their recreation in sledges of different shapes, such as tigers, swans, eagles, &c. In these the ladies sit dressed in velvet lined with furs, and adorned with laces and jewels, wearing on their heads a velvet cap; the sledge is drawn by one horse, set off with feathers, ribands, and bells; and as this diversion is chiefly taken in the night-time, footmen ride before the sledges with torches, and a gentleman, sitting on the sledge behind, guides the horse.—The Emperor, though an absolute sovereign in most of his hereditary dominions, is a limited monarch in regard to the empire. Almost every prince in the empire is arbitrary, being under very few restrictions in his German territories. The Emperor claims three sorts of dominion: That of Austria, as hereditary; Bohemia, as his right; and Hungary, by election. In his life-time he causes his son, or brother, or, failing of these, one of his nearest kinsmen, to be crowned King of Hungary, afterwards King of Bohemia, and then, if the electors are willing, he is chosen King of the Romans, whereby he is successor presumptive to the empire. The electors are, the Archbishops of Mentz, Triers, and Cologne, the king of Bohemia, the Duke of Bavaria, the Duke of Saxony, the King of Prussia, the Prince Palatine of the Rhine, and the King of Great Britain.

The
NORTH EAST
Part of
GERMANY

J.T. Scott sculp.

Odensee Zeeland Schonen BALTIC
Bornholm
Smolsin
Lauenberg
Rugen I. SEA
Lubeck POMERANIA Stetin Dantzick
Hamburg Holstein Camin
Elbe Lawenburg Stetin
LOWER Havelb. Pilnitz Thorn
Anger PRUSSIA
munde
Gardelegen BRANDENBURG
Magde- Castrin Frankford
SAXONY burg Berlin
Halberstadt Upper Crossen
Anhalt Wittenberg Glogau
Weissenfels Saxony Lusatia Oder
Thuringia Meissen Dresden Lusatia SILESIA Breslau
Leipsic Brieg
Weben Meissen Schweidnitz Dresden
Nareg Lelomeritz Troppau Teschen
Egra BOHEMIA
Prague Olmutz

NORTH-EAST PART OF GERMANY.

IN this divifion of Germany are *Pomerania, Brandenburgh*, and *Silefia*.—POMERANIA has the title of a Duchy; is bounded on the north by the Baltic Sea, on the eaft by Pruffia and Poland, on the fouth by the Marche of Brandenburg, and on the weft by the Duchy of Mecklenburg. One part of it belongs to the King of Pruffia, and the other to the Swedes. It is watered by feveral rivers, the principal of which are the Oder, the Pene, the Rega, and the Perfant. Though the air is cold, the foil is fruitful, abounding in paftures in fome places, and in others producing greater quantities of corn than are necefsary for the ufe of the inhabitants, who tranfport much of it into foreign countries. It is a flat country, containing many woods and forefts, and has feveral good harbours, particularly Stetin and Stralfund. It has fuffered greatly by wars, otherwife would have been much wealthier and more populous than it is at prefent. It is divided into the hither and farther Pomerania, and the river Pene divides the territories of the king of Sweden from thofe of the king of Pruffia.—BRANDENBURG is bounded on the north by Pomerania and Mecklenburgh; on the eaft, by Poland; on the fouth, by Silefia, Luface, and Magdeburg; and on the weft, by the territory of Lunenburg. The principal rivers are the Elbe, the Havel, the Sprey, and the Oder. Berlin, which is the capital of this electorate, and the refidence of the king of Pruffia, is a large, ftrong, and handfome city. The palace is magnificent, and there is a fine library, a rich cabinet of curiofities and medals, an academy of fci-

ences,

ences, and an obfervatory, befides a fuperb arfenal. Its trade and buildings have been lately much improved, and are every day growing more extenfive. A canal is cut from the river Sprey, to the Oder on the eaft, and another from thence to the Elbe on the weft.—SI-LESIA is bounded on the north by Brandenburg and Poland, on the fouth by Moravia and Hungary, on the eaft by Poland, and on the weft by lower Lufatia and Bohemia. The principal rivers are the Oder and the Viftula. There is a long chain of mountains, which feparate Bohemia from Silefia, one half belonging to the one, and the other half to the other. On the top of one of the mountains, called the giants, is a famous fpring, frequented by numbers of people, partly out of devotion, and partly to drink the waters. The higheft mountain of Silefia is called Zotenburg, fituated in the principality of Schweidnitz, and is 104 miles in circumference. Mines of gold and filver have been here difcovered; but thofe of gold have long fince ceafed to be worked, as they perhaps did not anfwer. There are alfo fome pecious ftones; but too much time is required to obtain them. The moft confiderable filver mines at prefent are at Reitftein, in the principality of Brieg. There are alfo mines of lead, copper, and iron, and quarries of various ftone; befides antimony, falt-petre, fulphur, alum, vitriol, quickfilver, fealed earth, and other minerals. The principal manufactory is linen cloth, and they have alfo fome woollen manufactories and glafs-houfes. They feed a great number of cattle, have large ftuds of horfes, and plenty of game in their woods.

The
NORTH WEST
Part of
GERMANY

J.T. Scott sculp. Philad.ª

GERMAN

Weser R.

Odense

DENMARK

BALTIC
SEA

Holstein Wag-
ria
Aubeck
Kiel

Stade
Harburg
Hamburg
Stormar
Wismar

Lewenburg

ELECT.r
Bremen
Lunenburg

Bremen

Lunen/

OF HANOVER

GERMAN

Oldenburg

Groningen

Slaven

OCEAN
Campen

Bishop.k
Hoy
Hoya
Hanover
Hildesheim
Brunswick

Bishop.k
Quinburg
Hameln

UPPER SAXONY

Zutphen

UNITED PROVINCES

Cleve

Munster
Wesel
Lipstat

Reclinghofen
Mark Westpha-
lia Cou. Walde-

Cassel

Waldeck
Gottingen

Landgrave
of Hesse

Cologne
Bonn
Juliars
Gintz

W. Weinstein
Cassel

S. Juns

NETHER
LANDS

Coblentz

Nassau

Marstein
Fuld

Scale of Miles 60 to a Deg.
40   40   60   80   100

No. 19.

NORTH-WEST PART OF GERMANY.

THE electorate of Hanover belongs to the king of
Great Britain. It has a capital of the same name,
which is agreeably situated in a sandy plain, in the circle of Lower Saxony. The elector resided here, before
he ascended the British throne, in a palace which makes
no great show outwardly, but within is richly furnished. The town is large and well built, and its fortifi-
cations are not indifferent. It suffered greatly by the
French, who got possession of it and the neighbouring
countries in the year 1757; but they were soon after
driven from thence. The regency here is administer-
ed in the same manner as if the sovereign was present.
The territory of Hanover at first comprehended nothing but the county of Lawenroad; but now it contains the duchy of Zell, Sax-Lawenburg, Bremen, Lunenburg, the principality of Verden, Grubenhagen, and
Oberwald George I. King of England, was the first that
gained possession of all these states, which lie mostly between the rivers Weser and Elbe. They produce timber, cattle, hogs, mum, beer, and bacon; a little silver,
copper, lead, iron, vitriol, brimstone, quicksilver; and
copperas; but these articles are not in such plenty as to
afford any considerable commerce.—OSNABURG is a bishopric in the circle of Westphalia. It is remarkable
that this bishopric is possessed by the papists and protes-
tants alternately, according to the tenor of the treaty at
Westphalia: The inspection and administration of ec-
clesiastical affairs belong to the elector of Cologne, as
metropolitan; but the civil affairs are always governed by the protestant bishop, in his turn. The air of

D 3   Westphalia

NORTH-WEST PART OF GERMANY.

Weftphalia is cold; but the foil produces pafture and fome corn, though there are many marfhes. The horfes here are large, and the hogs in high efteem, efpecially the hams which bear the name of this place. In this circle is the city of *Munfter*, whofe bifhop is one of the fovereign princes of the empire. It is defended by a ftrong citadel, which ftands diftinct from the city, and was free and imperial till 1661 : The citadel was built with a view to keep the inhabitants in awe. In 1533, a tailor, called John of Leyden, made himfelf mafter of the city, and drove away the bifhops and magiftrates; but it was taken from him three years afterwards, after a fiege of fourteen months, when he was tortured to death with red hot pincers.—HESSE-CASSEL is Landgraviate in the circle of the Upper Rhine. This country is furrounded with woods and mountains, in which are mines of iron and copper. In the middle, there are fome fine plains, fertile in corn and paftures, and there is plenty of all forts of fruits and honey. They likewife cultivate a large quantity of hops, which ferve to make excellent beer. Birch-trees are very common here, and they make a great deal of wine of the fap, which is faid to be very wholefome. It is fo populous that they can raife 30,000 men, without meddling with artificers, or thofe that till the ground. The Landgrave of Hefle-Caffel is an abfolute prince, and his revenues are faid to amount to 120,000l. per annum, befides what he makes by letting out his foldiers to any prince who will hire them, to be knocked on the head in wars, in which neither he nor they have the leaft concern.

20

8 5   8 7   8 9   9 1   9 3

Lou. E. from Philad.ª

SOUTH EAST
Part of
GERMANY

J.T. Scott sculp. Philadª

Scale of Miles 60 to a Deg.
20 40 60 80 100

S I L E S I A

R. Oder

Elb

Jung
Bunzlan   Glatz

Egra   Prague

Palot   K   of BOHEMIA   Frysberg
Pilsen   Olmutz

Bavaria   Tiseck   Pilgrim   MORAVIA
Taber   Iglaw   Brun

Ratisbon   Znaim

Hals

Du ELOF
B A V A R I A   Danube R.
Linz   Vienna

A D. of AUSTRIA

Munich   Wels
Waidock   Vogelberg   Neustat
Pruk

Ischen   B. of   S T Y R I A
Hall   SALTZBURG   Gratz
Insprag   Muldorf
B. of   Gemund   Isurk
Brixen   CARINTHIA   Windischgrack
Pierzen   Stain   Vacenfurt   Fridau
Gorilia   Chillei

I T A L Y   CARNIOLA
Czirnitz

Venice   Triest

GULF   of   VENICE

8 7   8 9   9 1   9 3

H U N G A R Y

SOUTH-EAST PART OF GERMANY.

IN this divifion is the kingdom of BOHEMIA, whofe capital is Prague, one of the largeft, fineft, and moft populous cities in Europe : It is twelve miles in circumference, and contains above an hundred churches, and as many palaces. The Moldaw flows through the middle of it, over which is a ftately ftone bridge. The air of this country is generally efteemed unwholefome, on account of the furrounding mountains not affording it a free paffage. The foil produces corn in plenty, the rivers are ftored with fifh, the woods with fowl, deer, and wild boars, and the pafture grounds are covered with tame cattle. In their mines are found gold, filver. iron, copper, and tin; but their principal manufacture is linen, of which they export great quantities by the Elbe. The Bohemian gentry are more inclined to arms than arts; and the boors or peafants, which are no better than flaves to their refpective lords, are faid to be a brutifh generation, and much given to pilfering and plundering their neighbours. The Marquifate of *Moravia* is a province annexed to the kingdom of Bohemia. It is a mountainous country, and watered by a great number of rivers and brooks. It takes its name from the river Morava, or Moraw, which runs through it, and is very fertile and populous. Hence the fect of Chriftians called Moravians, take their name, their doctrines having been firft broached here. Olmutz was formerly the capital city, but now Brinn claims that honour.—BAVARIA is a duchy, whofe duke is one of the electors of the empire. The principal rivers that flow through it are the

Danube, the Inn, the Ifer, and the Lech. The air is wholesome, and the foil fertile in wine, wheat, and good paftures; but the country in general, having little trade, is poor.—Austria excels all the provinces of Germany in the fertility of its foil, the plenty of its paftures, and the wholefomenefs of its air. Corn, wine, and fruit, are here in plenty, and their faffron is better than that of the Eaft-Indies. Vienna is the capital city of the circle of Auftria, and here the emperor refides. The city itfelf is not very large; but the fuburbs are fo extenfive, that in the whole it may contain about 600,000 inhabitants. The archducal treafury, and the cabinet of curiofities of the Houfe of Auftria, are as great rarities as any in the world; but, for a more particular defcription of thefe, as well as of the city of Vienna itfelf, we muft refer our readers to larger works.—Saltzberg belongs to the archbifhop of that name, who is a fovereign prince. It is populous, well built, and defended by a caftle, feated on a mountain. The archbifhop's palace is a fuperb ftructure, has a magnificent garden, adorned with ftatues, and planted with uncommon trees. This is his fummer houfe; but that for winter contains 163 apartments all richly furnifhed. Here are falt-works, which bring in a great revenue.—Carniola is a very confiderable province, and the moft fouthern one in this divifion. It is full of rocks and mountains, but produces corn, wine, and oil, and indeed every thing neceffary for the fupport of life.

SOUTH WEST
Part of
GERMANY
J.T.Scott sculp.

Scale of Miles

WESTPHALIA

U.RHINE

U.P. SAXONY

Rhine

D. OF
LUXEM-
BURG

Treves

Duck B. of
of Treves

Mentz

E.P. of
the Rhine

Wirtzburg

ONIA

Ohulbach

Nuremberg

Verdun

Thionville

Bitche

Nancy

Strasburg

St.Diev

Moselle

D. of
Wirtemberg

SWABIA

Danube

Augsburg

BAVA-
RIA

Turten-
berg

Kemplen

SWITZERLAND

FRANCE

SOUTH-WEST PART OF GERMANY.

THE palatine of the Rhine is not a very rich country, though there are very fine vineyards, fertile fields, handfome forefts, good gardens, and the rivers and lakes abound with fifh; they have plenty of cattle, game, and wild fowl, and good timber; however, there are neither mines nor faltworks. Its principal rivers are the Rhine and the Neckar, befides which there are feveral fmall ftreams. This province has fuffered more by the preceding wars with France, than any other of the provinces of Germany, the French having plundered the country, and demolifhed fome of its beft towns more than once.—LUXEMBURG lies in the foreft of Ardenne, which is one of the moft famous in Europe. In fome places it is covered with mountains and woods, but is in general fertile in corn and wine, and here are a great number of iron mines. The principal rivers are the Mofelle, the Sour, the Ourte, and the Semoy. It belongs partly to the houfe of Auftria, and partly to the French.—LORRAIN, like the former, is a Duchy, and abounds in all forts of corn, wine, hemp, flax, rape feed, game, and fifh. There are fine meadows, and large forefts, with mines of iron, filver, and copper, as alfo falt-pits. There are a great number of rivers, of which the Maefe, the Mofelle, and the Saar, are the principal. The inhabitants are laborious and valiant: They trade moftly among themfelves, having no navigable rivers by which they may extend their commerce: however, they have among themfelves all the neceffaries of life.—ALSACE is a very fertile country, producing plenty of corn, wine, pafture,

wood,

wood, flax, tobacco, pulfe, and fruit-trees. There are
mines of filver, copper, and lead, as well as mineral
waters. It is diverfified with pleafant hills, and mountains covered with forefts, in which are pine-trees 120
feet high. It is divided into the upper and lower, but
Strafburg is the capital of both.—In the circle of Swabia is the Duchy of Wurtemburg, through the middle
of which the Necker runs almoft from fouth to north.
Though there are many woods and mountains in it,
yet it is one of the moft populous and fertile countries
in Germany, producing plenty of paftures, corn, fruits,
and a great deal of wine towards the confines of the
palatinate. There are alfo mines and falt-fprings, with
plenty of game and fifh. Baden, is the capital of this
circle. Though a fmall, it is a handfome town, and
has its caftle fituated on the top of a mountain, where
the prince often refides. It is remarkable for its baths,
whence it takes its name, and is feated on the Rhine.
In Germany all the evils arifing from the antient feudal
fyftem, prevail very generally; while the few advantages that attended it, are no where to be found. The
princes, from the emperor to the moft inconfiderable
member of the diet are abfolute. Fond of military
parade, each of them fupports an eftablifiment of that
nature, to the utmoft extent of his revenue. The foldiers are alike the objects and the engines of oppreffi-
on; and while they fmart under the difcipline of the
moft arbitrary tyranny, they become the means of
riveting the chains of their fellow fubjects.

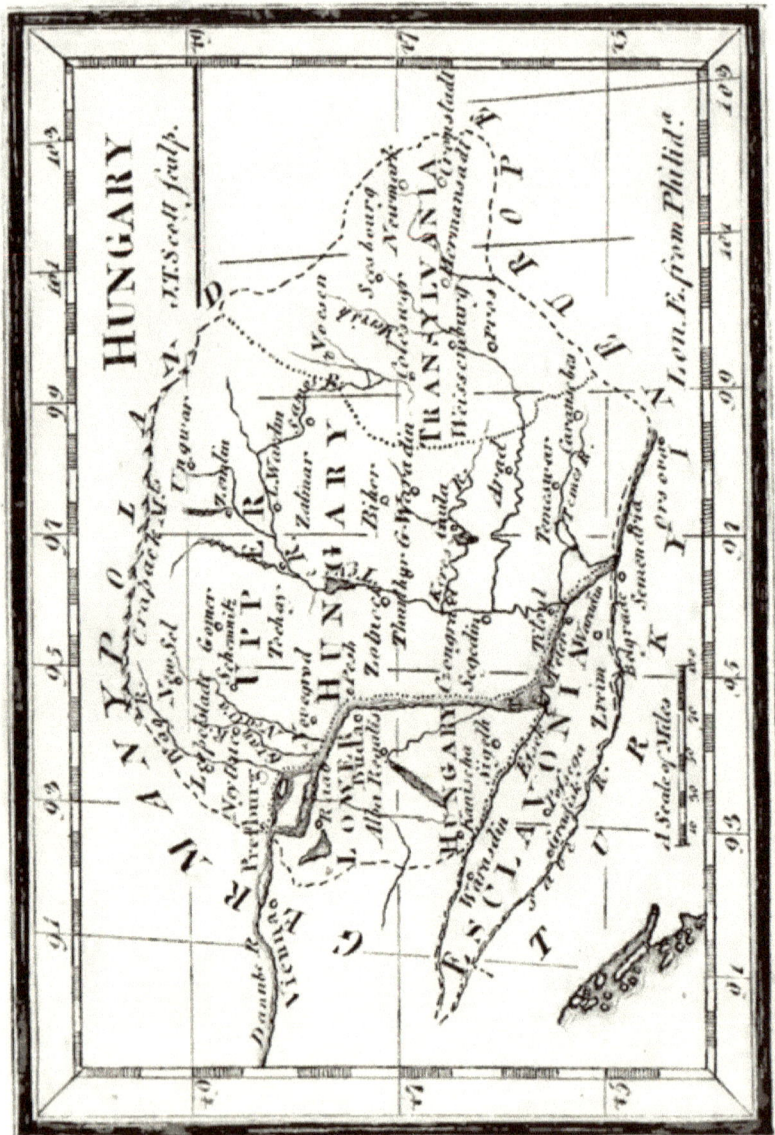

HUNGARY

J.H.Scott sculp.

POLAND

UPPER HUNGARY

LOWER HUNGARY

TRANSYLVANIA

GERMANY

ESCLAVONIA

TURKEY

A Scale of Miles

Long. E. from Phila.

HUNGARY.

HUNGARY is subject to the house of Austria, and is situated between 17° and 23° east longitude, and between 45° and 49° north latitude, being bounded by Poland on the north, by Transylvania on the east, by Sclavonia on the south, and by Austria and Moravia on the west. This kingdom is usually divided into upper and lower Hungary. The chief mountains are the Carpathian hills, which divide Hungary from Poland on the north; and the principal rivers the Danube, the Drave, the Save, and the Merish. The air of Hungary is very bad, occasioned by the numerous lakes and stagnant waters with which it abounds; but the country is one continued plain, extending upwards of three hundred miles, and producing plenty of corn, rich wines, and cattle: It abounds with game, deer, fish, and wild fowl, and in some parts are mines of silver, copper, and iron, besides salt. Their manufactures are principally those of brass and iron, of which they export a great deal wrought and unwrought. Hungary was a scene of war for upwards of two centuries, and is called the grave of the Germans, many thousands have perished in this unhealthy soil, as well by sickness as the sword. These people are of a good stature, and well proportioned. The men shave their beards, but leave whiskers on the upper lip; they wear fur caps on their heads, a close-bodied coat girt with a sash, and a short mantle over all, so contrived as to be buckled under the arm, and leave the right hand at liberty. The troopers wear a broad sword, and carry a hatchet, or battle-axe. The women also wear short

cloaks,

cloaks, and a veil when they go abroad; but the better fort imitate the French fashions. TRANSYLVANIA is likewife fubject to Auftria, is fituated between 22° and 26° caft longitude, and between 45° and 48° north latitude. It is bounded by the Carpathian mountains on the north, by the Irongate mountains on the eaft, by a part of Turkey on the fouth, and by Hungary on the weft. It is a very mountainous country, of which the Carpathian mountains on the north, and the Irongate mountains on the caft, are exceeding high and covered with fnow a great part of the year; the inland country is alfo mountainous and covered with woods, as the frontiers towards Turkey alfo are, from whence the Latin name of *Tranfylvania* was given to it The air is warm, but not fo unhealthy as that of Hungary, though the foil is much the fame. Their principal manufactures are copper and iron utenfils, but their foreign trade is very inconfiderable.—SCLAVONIA, like Hungary and Tranfylvania, is fubject to the houfe of Auftria. It is fituated between 16° and 22° caft longitude, and between 45° and 47° north latitude, being bounded by the river Drave on the north, by the Danube on the eaft, by the Save on the fouth, and by Stiria in Auftria on the weft. Sclavonia is a level country, not incumbered by woods or mountains, and is well watered by thofe fine navigable rivers, the Danube, the Drave, and the Save, befides other leffer ftreams, which render the foil exceeding fruitful, producing plenty of corn and wine, where it is properly cultivated. Thefe people are of a good ftature, a brave hardy race, and foldiers from their cradles, their country having formerly long been the feat of war.

HUNGARY.

cloaks, and a veil when they go abroad; but the better sort imitate the French fashions. TRANSYLVANIA is likewise subject to Austria, is situated between 22° and 25° east longitude, and between 45° and 48° north latitude. It is bounded by the Carpathian mountains on the north, by the Irongate mountains on the east, by a part of Turkey on the south, and by Hungary on the west. It is a very mountainous country, of which the Carpathian mountains on the north, and the Irongate mountains on the east, are exceeding high and covered with snow a great part of the year; the inland country is also mountainous and covered with woods, as the frontiers towards Turkey also are, from whence the Latin name of *Transylvania* was given to it. The air is warm, but not so unhealthy as that of Hungary, though the soil is much the same. Their principal manufactures are copper and iron utensils, but their foreign trade is very inconsiderable.—SCLAVONIA, like Hungary and Transylvania, is subject to the house of Austria. It is situated between 16° and 22° east longitude, and between 45° and 47° north latitude, being bounded by the river Drave on the north, by the Danube on the east, by the Save on the south, and by Stiria in Austria on the west. Sclavonia is a level country, not incumbered by woods or mountains, and is well watered by those fine navigable rivers, the Danube, the Drave, and the Save, besides other lesser streams, which render the soil exceeding fruitful, producing plenty of corn and wine, where it is properly cultivated. These people are of a good stature, a brave hardy race, and soldiers from their cradles, their country having formerly long been the seat of war.

POLAND

J.T.Scott sculp.

BALTIC SEA

GERMANY

GREAT POLAND

LIT. POLAND

RED POLAND

PODOLIA

VOLHINIA

LITHUANIA

SAMOGITIA

DUCHY OF

RUSSIA

HUNGARY

TURKY

LITTLE TARTARY

Lon.E.from Philad.t

Scale of Miles 69 to a Degree

POLAND.

POLAND is situated between 16° and 34° east longitude, and between 46° and 57° north latitude, being bounded by the Baltic Sea and Livonia on the north, by Ruffia on the eaft, by Turkey and Hungary on the fouth, and by Pomerania, Brandenburg, Silefia, and Moravia on the weft —The principal rivers in Poland are the Dwina, the Viftula, the Warta, and the Wilia.—The air of this country differs according to the nature and fituation of the different parts of the kingdom In the provinces towards the north weft it is very cold, though pure and wholefome; but towards the north-eaft it is not only cold, but very grofs and unwholefome The north-weft provinces are very fertile, affording many forts of grain and fruits, not only enough for the inhabitants, but alfo to fupply the wants of their neighbours. In the middle part of this kingdom are fome mountains well ftored with feveral mines of filver, copper, iron, and lead; but the provinces towards the north and north-eaft are very barren in fruits and corn, being full of woods, lakes, and rivers.—Thefe people trouble themfelves very little with traffic, but leave it to the city of Dantzic, and other port towns on the Viftula and Baltic. Dantzic is a free hanfeatic town, governed by its own laws, and its own magiftrates, and all extraordinary affairs are decided by the council; but if any thing very important happens, it is carried before the grand chancellor of Poland, or the diet.—The Polanders are handfome, tall, well-proportioned men, of good and durable complexions, and of fuch ftrong and vigorous conftitu-

tions,

POLAND.

tions, that many of them prove the beft of foldiers, being able to endure all the fatigues of a military life. They are generally reckoned very affable and courteous to ftrangers, extremely jealous of their liberties and privileges; but moft tyrannical to the meaneft fort of the people, treating the peafants as no better than mere flaves, and in fome places exercife a power of life and death upon their domeftic fervants.—The Conftitution of Poland not only refembles a republic, but is really fuch; for the legiflative power is lodged in the ftates, and the executive power in the fenate, of which the king is only prefident, when he is prefent, and they can meet and confult without him. The king is elected by the clergy and gentry in the plains of Warfaw; and if the minority fhould be fo hardy as to infift on their diffent, they generally determine their difpute with their fwords.—What we have now faid of the conftitution of Poland, our readers muft confider as a fhort defcription of what it was, rather than that of what it now is, or likely to be again. Pruffia, Ruffia, and the emperor fome years back feized on the moft delightful and valuable part of Poland from them. The poorer part of the inhabitants could not be fufferers, fince they could not fubmit to more cruel and tyrannical mafters than they experienced in their own nobles.

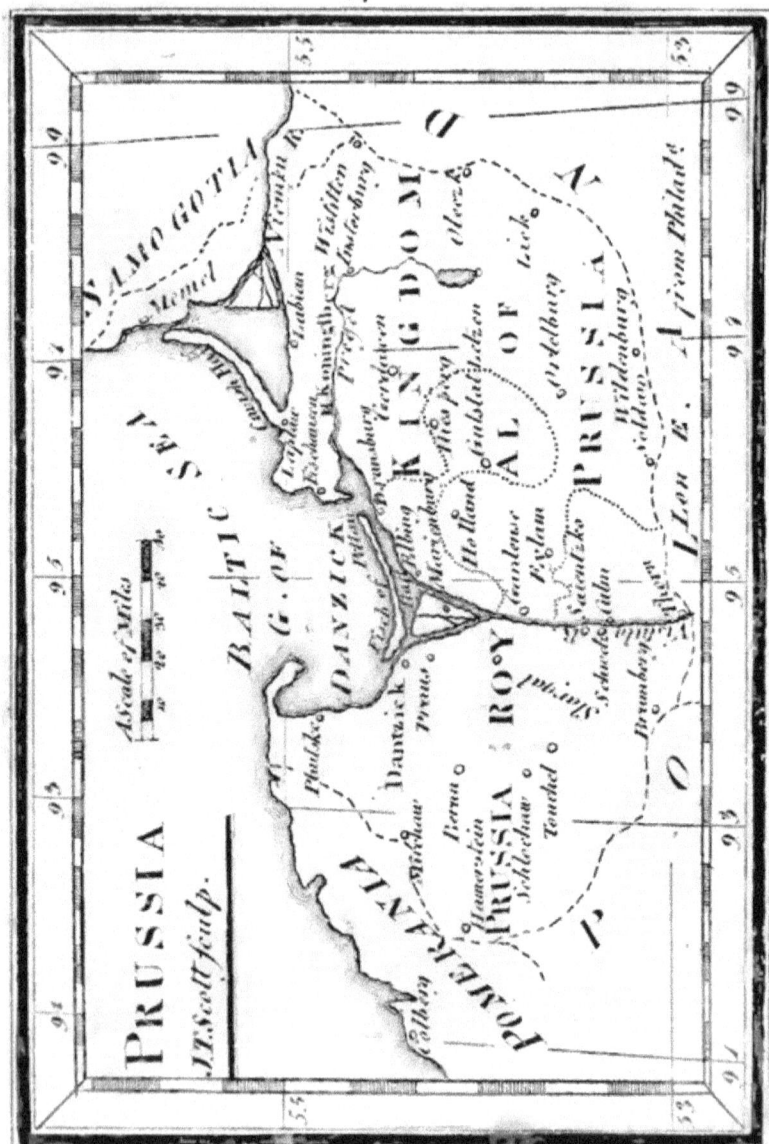

PRUSSIA

J.T.Scott Sculp.

Scale of Miles

SAMOGOTIA

BALTIC SEA

G. OF DANZICK

KING DOM

AL OF PRUSSIA

ROYL PRUSSIA

POMERANIA

Lon. E. from Philad?

Memel

Niemen R.

Danzick

Thorn

PRUSSIA.

IT will not be eafy to give the latitude and longitude of his Pruffian majefty's dominions, which are fo much detached from each other, without running into a length inconfiftent with the brevity of our prefent plan. Suffice it to fay, that the kingdom of Pruffia is about 400 miles long, and in fome parts about 160 broad. The Brandenburg, or Ducal Pruffia, was, in the beginning of this century, erected into a kingdom, when Frederick III. elector of Brandenburg, was crowned the firft king of Pruffia. The Polifh, or Royal Pruffia, is that part which borders upon Great Poland and Pomerania, containing the diftricts of Marienburg and Calm, and the bifhopric of Ermeland. To Brandenburg, or Ducal Pruffia, which is that part all along the Baltic up to Courland, belong the three provinces of Sameland, Nataugen, and Pomerania. Pruffia, is for the moft part, a very fruitful country, producing flax, hemp, and corn. There are a great number of domeftic animals, befides game, which is very common; and the fea, rivers, and lakes, fupply them with great plenty of fifh. Befides the common game, there are elks, wild affes, and uri, in the forefts : Thefe laft are of a monftrous fize, and have fome refemblance to the beeves. Their hides are extremely thick and ftrong, and they fell them to foreigners at a great price. There are alfo mountains of white fand, covered with oaks and pines, and there they find a vifcous fubftance, which, being expofed to the air, turns to a yellow amber; but the greateft part proceeds from the fea; when the wind begins to blow, the peafants run

to

to the fhore, and fifh for amber with great iron rakes, of which the whiteft is in the higheft efteem. There are two large lakes, befides the rivers Viftula and Pregel. The inhabitants are of a good conftitution, laborious, robuft, and are now undoubtedly the beft trained foldiers in the world, the rigour of the military difcipline being inconceivable.

In Pruffia, defpotifm affumes all its horrors. The wretched inhabitants are wholly at the difpofal of the king. Whatever number of fons a peafant may have, they are all taken into the army, except one; who is left to affift in managing the farm; the reft wear badges from their childhood, to mark that they are deftined to be foldiers, and obliged to enter into the fervice when called upon. The late king endeavoured to increafe the commerce of the kingdom, but the nature of his defpotic government was not favourable to trade, there are, however, a number of mechanics; but the principal bufinefs of the inhabitants is hufbandry, and feeding of cattle.

DENMARK

A Scale of Miles 60 to a Deg.
20   30   40   50   60

SCHAGER or CAPE CAT Te

P.t or Sw DEN

Schagen

Kellen

Alburg

Holme

Wilburg

Holsteire

Ripen

Arenhusen

Odense

Funen

Stes

wick

Stormar   Wagria

The Sound

Haslem

Betwen

COPENHAGEN

Zeeland

Korsor

Hogemp

Langeland

BALTIC
SEA

Rostock

P.t or   GERMANY

Longitude East 10 from London

DENMARK.

THE kingdom of Denmark is situated between 8°
and 13° east longitude, and between 54° and 58°
north latitude. It is bounded by the Scaggerac Sea,
which divides it from Norway, on the north; by the
Sound, which divides it from Sweden, on the east; by
Germany and the Baltic, on the south; and by the German ocean, which divides it from Great Britain, on the
west. As this is a flat country, abounding in bogs and
morasses and surrounded by the sea, it is extremely subject to fogs and foul-air. Zealand, which is the principal island, and the seat of government, affords a very
indifferent soil. No wheat will grow here, and good
pasture is very scarce: Great part of it is a forest, and
reserved for the King's game. Funen, the next largest
island, produces hardly corn sufficient for its inhabitants.—As to their habits, they usually imitate the
French dress; but in winter they wrap themselves up
in furs and wool, like their neighbours. Few of them
have an extensive genius, nor are they expert at inven-
tion or imitation, being neither deeply learned, nor excellent mechanics. Excessive drinking is a vice to which
they are much addicted; and the common people are
said to be poor spirited wretches, having nothing of the
remains of the bravery or enterprizing genius of their
ancestors.—Before the year 1660, the legislative power
was lodged in the states of Denmark, and the executive
power in the senate, of which the king was no more
than president. In time of war, indeed, he was comman-
der in chief of the sea and land forces; but he could
neither raise men or money, or make peace or war,

E   without

DENMARK.

without the concurrence of the flates. At prefent however, the king of Denmark is abfolute.—Copenhagen,
which is the capital of this kingdom, is a large, rich,
and ftrong city, and has an Univerfity. A new palace
was built here in 1730, which is very magnificent. In
the *Mufeum Regium*, is a curious reprefentation, by iron
wire, of the veins and arteries of the human body, all
of them appearing in their natural fituation, bignefs,
and colour : An artificial human fkeleton of ivory ; his
right hand grafps a large fcythe, and the left holds a
fand-glafs : A model of a fhip, with the mafts and fails,
all of ivory : And a cabinet of ivory and ebony, very
beautiful and admirably well contrived within, which
is faid to be the work of a Danifh mechanic quite blind.
The arfenal is furnifhed with naval ftores fufficient at
any time to fupply a large fleet ; and the citadel is a
regular fort, defended by five good baftions, a double
ditch full of water, and feveral advanced works. The
exchange of the Eaft-India company, the arfenal, the
king's ftables, the college, the opera and orphan houfes,
are all fuperb ftructures. The royal library contains
above 40,000 manufcripts, and printed books collected
from all parts. Copenhagen is above five miles in circumference, and is feated on the eaftern fhore of the
ifle of Zealand, upon a fine bay of the Baltic Sea, near
the ftraits called the Sound. Denmark has very little
cafh in it, which is principally owing to the officers of
the army, being ufually foreigners, who, if they fave
any money, place it in foreign banks ; and this is likewife practifed by their minifters. Befides this, the balance of trade, being againft them, carries off much of
their money.

SWEDEN and NORWAY
NORTHERN OCEAN
NORWEGIAN SEA
Gulf of Bothnia
A Scale of Miles
References

SWEDEN AND NORWAY.

SWEDEN (part of the ancient Scandinavia, which comprehended Sweden, Denmark and Norway) is bounded by Norwegian Lapland on the north; by Rusfia, on the eaft; by the Baltic Sea, which divides it from Germany, on the fouth; and by the feas called the Sound and Scaggerac, with the Dofrine hills, which divide it from Denmark and Norway, on the weft.— Stockholm is the capital of this kingdom, and the ordinary refidence of the king: It is built on fix fmall iflands, which are joined together by wooden bridges. The city makes a grand appearance, having many ftately palaces covered with copper. The harbour is very large, but dangerous to approach, on account of the rocks and cliffs that are feen in the fea for 48 miles together.—Sweden is a very cold country, their hills being always covered with fnow. Moft of the inhabitants lie under ground to fhelter themfelves from the winds, which blow here in a terrible manner. They have neither fpring nor autumn: They have fummer, however, for three months, which comes fo quick upon them that the vallies are all green in a few days, which before were covered with fnow; and in that fhort feafon they fow and plant all manner of kitchen herbs. They have little corn land, but good pafture, and plenty of venifon and fifh: The rein-deer, of which there are abundance, are very ufeful creatures; for they draw the inhabitants long journies in fledges, give them milk to drink, flefh to eat, and fkins for clothing. —The Swedes are men feemingly formed by nature for foldiers: As to arts and fciences they make no

E 2

figure

SWEDEN AND NORWAY.

figure in them, being more inclined to fit down with a
fuperficial knowledge of things, than to purfue their
ftudies to any degree of perfection.

NORWAY is bounded by the Frozen Ocean, on the
north; by Sweden and Ruffia, on the eaft; by the
Scaggerac Sea, which feparates it from Denmark, on
the fouth; and by the Atlantic Ocean, on the weft.—
There are feveral iflands fubject to Norway; among
them, the moft noted is the Ifle of Iceland, which lies
600 miles weftward from Norway. Here during two
months in fummer the fun never fets, and in the winter
it never rifes above the herizon for the fame fpace.
Iceland is noted for its volcano called Mount Hecla,
which fometimes throws out torrents of fire. The inhabitants have neither corn-fields, vineyards, nor gardens to cultivate, but for their living are obliged to
fpend their time in hunting and fifhing. They dry
their fifh, and melt their fat, which afterwards they
fell to other nations. They have good horfes, which
fometimes, for the want of hay or grafs, are forced to
feed upon ftock-fifh. The people are not very fond
of money, but rather barter their commodities for
bread, wine, brandy, flour, &c.—As to the prefent
ftate of Norway, that part next to Denmark is well
peopled; but farther towards the north it is a perfect
wildernefs, full of mountains, and exceffively cold.
The heft produce of this country is the fifhery, efpecially that of ftock-fifh, which are fent all over Europe.
As this kingdom abounds with forefts, it has a great
deal of timber, deals, and oaks, of which England and
Holland take a prodigious quantity every year. Norway belongs to Denmark, and is governed by a viceroy.

RUSSIA
in
EUROPE

A Scale of Miles
100 200 400

NOVA Zembla

NORTHERN OCEAN

References
a. Kargapol
b. Rosten
c. Sousdel
d. Woldimer
e. Lachine

Mosco: Lapland

C. Candenois

Petzora
or
Boran day

Artic Cir.

White Sea

Kolmogord
skia

Great Permia

G. of Bothnia

St. PETERSBURG

G. of Finland

Ingria

Nov
gorod

Livo-Ples

Plakow

Rzeva

Moscowa

Vaitka

Scher
mitsa

CASAN

Riga

Koningsberg

f. Biela
g. Smolinske
h. Severia
i. Rezan

POLAND

Lit:
Novo
gorod

Little
Russia

Saratof

PART OF

RUSSIA

Kiow

Pultowa

Don
Cossacs
Izof

Astrakan

Guriengorod

Oczakow

LITTLE
TARTARY

CAS
PIAN
SEA

Krim

BLACK SEA

RUSSIA IN EUROPE.

THIS extensive empire is situated between 23° and 65° east longitude, and between 47° and 72° north latitude, being bounded by the Frozen Ocean on the north, by Asiatic Russia on the east, by Little Tartary and Turkey on the south, and by Poland, the Baltic Sea, and Sweden, on the west.—The principal rivers in Russia are the Wolga, the Oby, the Boristhenes, the Dwina, and the Cam.—Russia is generally marshy, full of forests, lakes, and rivers, and in the eastern and northern parts it is extremely cold, and but thinly peopled; but those parts towards Poland are in a more temperate climate, and consequently more fruitful and populous. This country affords salt, brimstone, pitch, tar, hemp, flax, iron, steel, and copper. The Russian leather is very much valued in Europe; and here furs are in great plenty, which are not only worn by the inhabitants, but other countries are furnished with them from hence.—This large country is under the dominion of one monarch, who governs with absolute sway, and was commonly stiled *Czar of Muscovy*, till Peter the Great assumed the title of *Emperor of all Russia*. The present Empress of Russia has distinguished herself by the favour and patronage she bestows on learned and ingenious men, and by giving the greatest encouragement to arts and commerce. She has also distinguished herself in other matters not quite so laudable. The whole of her empire is said to form a square, whose sides are 2000 miles each; great part of which is in a state of barbarism. Instead of seeking true glory, by properly improving this immense empire, she

is

RUSSIA IN EUROPE.

is employed in war to enlarge it. The method of travelling in Rusfia Lapland is in fledges drawn by rein-
deer, the fnow being frozen hard enough to bear them.
Thefe deer run as faft as a race-horfe, flying in a manner from one hill of fnow to another. In the middle of
Rusfia they travel alfo in fledges, but drawn by horfes.
The fledge-way is beft beaten in February, when they
travel night and day in a kind of coaches fixed on fledges, fo expeditioufly, that they go from Peterfburg to
Mofcow, which are more than 400 miles diftant, in
three days and three nights, there being a convenient
place in the coach to lie down and fleep. It is very
remarkable, that partridges, hares, foxes, and fome
other animals, turn white in the northern provinces
during the winter.—The Rusfians are of a good ftature,
and inclinable to be corpulent; their features and complexions are good, and they have hale, vigorous con-
ftitutions. The Laplanders, who inhabit the coaft of
the Frozen Ocean, are of the Tartar make, and clothe
themfelves from head to foot in the fkins of their rein-
deer, fewing two fkins together, fo that they have the
hair next them, as well as on the outfide, their coat
and cap being all of a piece. Inftead of a fhirt, they
wear a waiftcoat made of a young fawn's fkin, which
keeps them warm.—Peterfburg, which is the capital of
this empire, is a large handfome city, built by Peter
the Great in 1703. It is of a prodigious extent, and
is feated on an ifland, which lies in the middle of the
river Neiva, where the land has been confiderably raifed. The fort is very ftrong, and is a regular fortification; but the principal defect of this city is, that it
is not built high enough to protect it from inundation.
The forces of this empire are very great.

RUSSIA P.t OF

TURKY in EUROPE

P.t OF

TURKY IN ASIA

BLACK SEA

LITTLE TARTARY

Crim

ANATOLIA

GERMANY P.t OF POLAND

Moldavia

Wallachia

Bulgaria

Romania

Servia

Bosnia

Dalmatia

Albania

Macedonia

Adrianople

Archipelago

P.t OF VENICE

GULF OF VENICE

ITALY

Sicily I.

Candia I.

MEDITERRANEAN SEA

A Scale of Miles

No. 28.

TURKEY IN EUROPE.

THIS country is fituated between 17° and 40° eaſt longitude, and between 36° and 46° north latitude, being bounded on the north by Ruſſia, Poland, and Sclavonia ; on the caſt, by Circaſſia, the Black Sea, the Propontis, the Hellefpont, and the Archipelago; on the fouth, by the Mediterranean Sea; and on the weſt, by the fame fea, and the Venetian and Auſtrian territories. —Conſtantinople, which is the capital of Turkey in Europe, is the fineſt port in Europe; it has a delight-ful fituation in point of profpect, and the noble anti-quities it contains are fcarcely to be equalled. That part of it, which is called the city, is twelve miles in circumference, and the fuburbs are at leaſt of equal dimenſions, the whole computed to contain two milli-ons of people. The city being of a triangular figure, the feraglio is built upon the point of one of the an-gles, which runs out between the Propontis and the harbour ; and below the palace, upon the declivity of the hill, are the gardens, lying on the water : From hence is a delightful view of the beautiful coaſt of the Leſſer Aſia, and the Seraglio of Scutari. The mofque of St. Sophia, once a Chriſtian church, is faid, in many refpects, to excel that of St. Peter in Rome.—The pre-fent ſtate, foil, produce, &c. of Turkey in Europe, are the fame as Turkey in Aſia, of which we ſhall fpeak hereafter.—The principal Grecian iſlands are divided into four claſſes, viz. the iſlands of Candia, the Negro-pont, the Ionic iſlands, and the iſlands in the Archipe-lago. Befides thefe there are a great number of other iſlands of lefs note; among which is that of Rhodes, at

E 4   the

the mouth of whofe harbour once ftood the coluffus cf brafs, efteemed one of the wonders of the world : One foot of it was placed on one fide of the harbour, and the other foot on the other fide, fo that fhips paffed between its legs : The face of this Coluffus reprefented the fun, to whom it was dedicated. The height of it was about 135 feet, and it held in one hand a light-houfe for the direction of fhips.—The air of Greece, being generally pure and temperate, is reckoned very pleafant and healthful. The foil is not only fit for pafture, but alfo affords plenty of grain, and abounds with excellent grapes and delicious fruits. The antient Greeks were juftly celebrated as excelling all others in arts and arms. The prefent form a direct contraft. Such is the preffure of the Ottomon yoke, under which they groan, that their fpirits are quite funk, and their very afpect declares a difconfolate and dejected mind. However, the unthinking part of them fo little confider their prefent flavifh fubjection, that there is no people more jovial and merrily difpofed, being fo much given to finging and dancing, that is is now become a proverbial faying, *As merry as a Greek.* Such has been the hard fate of this country, that fcarce a trace of its former glory and grandeur are now to be perceived.

NAPLES and SICILY

THE ADRIATIC SEA or GULF OF VENICE

Pome I.o   Lissa I.

St Andrew

Abruzzo
Aquila
Ultra

Abruzzo
Citra

Trémiti I.

Manfredonia

Bari
Proxi
Bari

VENICE

Brindisi

Otranto

Taranto

MEDITERRANEAN
SEA

C. Palinure

Calabria Citra

A Scale of Miles 60 to a Degree
20 40 60 80 100

Lipari Islands

Lipari I.

Stromboli

Calabria Ultra

S. Severina

C. Rizzuto

Stilo

Palermo

Messina
Catania
M. Etna

C. Spartivento

C. dell'Armi

Mazara

SICILY I.

Leontini

Alicata

Noto

Syracusa

C. Passaro

NAPLES AND SICILY.

THE kingdom of NAPLES is a fort of peninfula, and is bounded on three fides by the Mediterranean Sea, and on the north by the territories of the Pope. The Appenine Mountains crofs the whole country from eaft to weft, and divide it into two parts — The foil contains a great mixture of fulphur, of which there are many mines. The heat of the country is greatly owing to this, and for the fame reafon the fruits become perfectly ripe. There are oranges, lemons, citrons, pomegranates, almonds, dates, capers, and figs : befides fugar, pepper, and manna. The wine produced here is excellent. This country is not lefs rich in flax, hemp, oil, olives, honey, wax, &c Deer, fifh, and fowls, are very plenty. The Neapolitan horfes are in high efteem.—The Neapolitans who live in the country are very fond of hunting; but thofe in the city pafs their time in going to fhews and fpectacles. The ladies are generally addicted to gallantry.—The city of Naples is one of the fineft in the world : It is feated on the fea coaft, furrounded with thick walls, regular baftions, ftrong towers, deep ditches, and feveral fortified caftles. The ftreets are large, ftraight, and paved with freeftone. The Bay of Naples is highly celebrated.

The ifland of SICILY is divided from Italy, by the narrow ftrait of Meffina, which is not feven miles over. The moft noted mountain in this ifland is that of Etna, now called Gibella, a terrible volcano, fituate in the province of Val Demona. This mountain is fixty miles in circumference, and 10,954 feet in height; its fiery

eruptions

eruptions have always rendered it famous; it ſtands ſeparate from all other mountains; the lower parts of Mount Etna are very fruitful in corn and ſugar canes, the middle abounds with woods, and the upper part is almoſt the whole year covered with ſnow. Any conſiderable eruption is generally preceded by an earthquake. The mountain throws out pumice-ſtone, &c. in great abundance for a conſiderable time; at length a torrent of liquid fire overflows at ſome of the former craters, or forces for itſelf a new paſſage high up the mountain, and flowing down it, ruſhes into the ſea, ſpreading the moſt fatal deſolation in its courſe. The town of Catania was overturned by an earthquake in 1693, and 18,000 people were ſaid to be deſtroyed with it. Syracuſe, once the capital of this iſland, has been ſo often demoliſhed by them, that very little of it remains at preſent.—The air of this country, from the warmth of its climate, is healthful, being refreſhed from every ſide by the ſea breezes.—The hills and vallies are exceeding fruitful, and produce plenty of corn, wine, oil, and ſilk; with which laſt article they carry on a very extenſive commerce.—Palermo is the capital of this iſland, and was the ſeat of the ancient kings It is a place of great trade; the ſtreets are handſome, the houſes ſuperb, well fortified, and very populous. There is a magnificent caſtle built near the ſea-ſide, where the Viceroy (who governs under the King of Naples, to whom the whole iſland belongs) uſually reſides ſix months in the year; and his preſence draws a great number of nobility to this place.

TURKY IN ASIA

J.T.Scott sculp.

Scale of Miles 60 to a Deg.

TURKEY IN ASIA.

THIS extenfive country is fituated between 27° and 45° eaft longitude, and between 28° and 45° north latitude; being bounded on the north by the Black Sea and Circaffia; on the eaft, by Perfia; on the fouth, by Arabia and the Levant Sea; and on the weft, by the Archipelago, the Hellefpont, and Propontis.—The principal mountains are Olympus, Taurus, Arrarat, Lebanon, and Ida.—The rivers moft worthy of notice, are the Euphrates, the Tigris, the Orantes, the Sarabat, and the Jordan. The climate of this empire, in general, is very temperate : They are not often incommoded by frofts, nor fcorched with exceffive heats, and yet the air is not healthful : The plague vifits the empire once in four or five years; and in the year 1773, in only two cities, Bagdat, and Baffora, it is faid to have fwept away not lefs than 400,000 of their inhabitants. If we may add to this number thofe that have fallen by the fword, and by other accidents, in the courfe of the fame year, in their campaign againft the Ruffians, what an idea muft we form of that empire, which can fuftain fuch confiderable loffes without any apparent diminution of her ftrength! The principal caufe that the plague is fo exceedingly deftructive arifes from their want of caution to guard againft it; they go frequently into houfes where they know the plague is; and even put on, without cleaning, the clothes of thofe recently dead of that infectious difeafe; for, as the doctrine of predeftination prevails in Turkey, they think it in vain to endeavour to avoid their fate.— Turkey is advantageoufly fituated in a fruitful foil, producing

ducing excellent wool, corn, wine, oil, fruit, coffee, rhubarb, myrrh, and other odoriferous plants and drugs, in the greatest variety and abundance; but the Turks are generally above applying themfelves to manufactures, thefe being chiefly managed by the Chriftians, who annually export from thence the fineft carpets, befides great quantities of cotton, leather, raw filk, &c.--The Grand Signior, or Emperor of the Turks, is reftrained by no law, and the people, as well as the country, are confidered as his property : Every man's life and fortune in the empire is at his difpofal.—It is generally obferved that the Turks are perfonable men, which may proceed from the choice they make of their women. They collect the greateft beauties that can be met with in the neighbouring countries, and thefe principally from the Grecian territories, which are faid to produce the fineft women in the world. Polygamy is general. The good Muffulman is allowed by his religion to have four wives, and as many concubines as he pleafes. The generality of the Turks love a flothful and indolent life, and faunter away their time either among the women in the haram, or in fmoaking, or taking opium; and though they herd together, you will obferve as little converfation among them, as among fo many inanimate beings; they have little curiofity in enquiring into the ftate of other nations. The early Turks, fired by enthufiafm, were valiant to excefs; and their defcendants, however indolent, do not want courage.

PERSIA

J.T. Scott sculp.

References
a. *Ghilan*
b. *Tabristan*
c. *Counus*
d. *Astrabad*
e. *Esferain*
f. *Tabasin*

RUS

Geor

Caspian Sea

Aral L.

Uryeyz Bokam

Aran U. BEEK TARTARS

Amouye

Hider Marou Cage Han Termed

Coraſan Cotton Balk

Ghizan Sevas

Susa

Perſian Couheſtan Hegi

Shahi Hamadan Hasab

Baghad Irak Tabas Zure L.

Suster Feria Herra

Khuzef Segeſtan Tahiend

Basra Darac Sableſtan

Farſiſtan Damrabeb

Shiras Keresſan

Gomgon Laveſtan Bam

Mo goſ Mecran

Perſian Gulf

ARABIA

PERSIAN SEA

Scale of Miles 60 to a Deg.
100 300 600

PERSIA.

THE kingdom of Perſia is ſituated between 45° and 67° eaſt longitude, and between 25° and 45° north latitude; being bounded on the north, by Circaſſia, the Caſpian Sea and Uſbec Tartary; on the eaſt, by Eaſt India; on the ſouth, by the Indian Ocean and the Gulf of Perſia; and on the weſt, by Turkey.—There is no country in Aſia that abounds more with mountains, or has fewer rivers, than Perſia. The mountains of Caucaſus and Arrarat fill all the iſthmus between the Euxine and Caſpian Seas : Thoſe called Taurus, and the ſeveral branches thereof, run through Perſia, from Natolia to India, and fill all the middle of the country. The principal rivers are the Oxus and the Indus.—On the mountains of Caucaſus and Dagiſtan, which are frequently covered with ſnow, the air is cold, and on the tops of other mountains much colder ; but their vallies are very unhealthful. The middle of Perſia, however, is much admired for the pureneſs and ſerenity of the air, the ſtars ſhining ſo exceeding bright, that ſome travellers relate, that they could ſee to read by their light. —The ſoil of Perſia is in general very barren; but, where they can turn the water into the plains, it is not unfruitful : It produces great quantities of wine and oil, ſenna, rhubarb, and other drugs, with various ſorts of delicious fruits, and ſome corn. Their manufactures are thoſe of ſilk, woollen, mohair, carpets, and leather.—Perſia is an abſolute monarchy, the lives and eſtates of the people being entirely at the diſpoſal of their prince, who has no eſtabliſhed council, but is adviſed by ſuch miniſters as are moſt in favour.—It is no
wonder

PERSIA.

wonder that the Persians are of a good stature, shape, and complexion, since, like the Turks, they plunder all the neighbouring nations for beautiful women.—They wear large turbans on their heads, and some of them are very rich, being interwoven with gold and silver. They wear a vest, girt with a sash, and over it a loose garment something shorter, and sandals or slippers on their feet. When they ride, which they do often, they wear pliant boots of yellow leather, and the furniture of their horses is immoderately rich, the stirrups being always of silver. The dress of the women does not differ much from that of the men, excepting that their vests are longer, and they wear a stiffened cap on their heads, and their hair down.—The Persians have always been esteemed a brave people, of great vivacity and quick parts; but are framed for nothing more than their humanity and hospitality. Their greatest foibles are profuseness and vanity; the richness of their clothes, and number of their servants and equipage, too often exceed their revenues, and bring them into difficulties.—They have a prodigious number of birds of prey, and no people are better instructed how to take them than the Persians: Their hawks are taught not only to fly at birds, but at hares. They excel in writing, and have eight several hands: They write from the right hand to the left, as the Arabs do.—The Persians drink coffee for breakfast, and at eleven they dine upon melons, fruits, or milk; but their chief meal is in the evening, when they usually have a dish of boiled rice, with fowls or mutton, so overdone that they pull the meat in pieces with their fingers, using neither knives, forks, nor spoons.

INDIA
on both Sides the
GANGES

Lon. E. from Philada.

Lon. W.

CHINA

TIBET

PERSIA

MOGULS EMPIRE

Dehli

Agra

Talla

Patna

Bengal

Bay of Bengal

Deccan

Golconda

Malabar

Goa

Ceylon

INDIAN OCEAN

Scale of Miles to a Deg.

BENGAL

Andaman Is.

Nicobar I.

Malacca

Str. of Malacca

Sumatra I.

Achem

G. of Cochinchina

C. Henry

Borneo

Str. of Siam

Ava

K. of Arakan

C. Comorin

H. Scott sculp.

No. 31.

INDIA ON BOTH SIDES THE GANGES.

THAT immense tract called the East Indies is situated between 66° and 109° east longitude, and between 1° and 40° north latitude; being bounded on the north by part of Persia, Tibet, and China; on the south, by the Indian Ocean; on the west, by the same ocean and Persia; and on the east, by the Pacific Ocean.—We shall speak first of INDIA *within the Ganges*, or the empire of the Great Mogul, whose chief mountains are those of Caucasus, Naugracut, and Balagate; which last run almost the whole length of India, from north to south: They are so high, and covered with such forests, that they stop the western monsoons, (which are periodical winds) the rains beginning a month sooner on the Malabar coast than they do on the eastern coast of Coromandel.—The principal rivers are the Indus, the Ganges, and the Christiana.—As this country extends through a great many climates, the air consequently must be very different in the southern provinces from what it is in the northern. The northern and midland provinces of India enjoy a fine, serene, temperate air, while those in the south are parched with heat some months in the year, particularly in April and May, when the hot winds blow for two or three hours in the morning with a scorching heat, coming over a long tract of burning sand for several hundred miles; but about noon the sea breezes arise and refresh the natives. Their principal fruit-trees are the palm, cocoa-nut, tamarind, mango, pine-apple, pomegranate, orange and lemon. The country also produces rice, wheat, pepper, and a great quantity of garden-stuff.—Their

. animals

INDIA ON BOTH SIDES THE GANGES.

animals are numerous, among which are the elephant, camel, horses, oxen, and a variety of wild beasts.—Their manufactures are principally of muslins, callicoes, and silks, with which we are supplied in great quantities from Bengal, the capital of the English settlements in India.—The Mogul is an absolute prince, and his revenues are computed at forty millions sterling per annum.—The complexions of the inhabitants are no less various than their climate, being black, white, and tawney. They are a very ingenious people, hospitable and benevolent.—The air of INDIA *beyond the Ganges* is dry and healthful in the north; but the southern provinces, being very hot and moist, especially in the vallies and low lands near the sea, are not near so healthy. However, here they build most of their towns, their houses standing upon high pillars, to secure them from the floods, during which season they have no communication with each other but by boats; and such storms of wind, thunder, and lightning, happen about the equinoxes, on the shifting of the monsoons, as are seldom felt in Europe.—The soil of Tonquin has been gradually formed by the mud, which the river leaves behind, and makes the earth exceeding fruitful as far as it extends. All the higher grounds are dried up and burnt by the sun soon after the rains are over. —The government of Tonquin is very particular: The king enjoys only the name, and the prime minister has all the power, to whom every one makes his court. In fact, the king is but a prisoner of state, and is shown only once a year to his subjects.

EAST INDIA ISLANDS
J.T.Scott sculp.
Havnan I.
PHILIPPINE
Manilla I.
Parcel Shoals
Manilla Is.
Mindora
Taudaya
Lawta
CAROLINE Is.
Paragoa
Bansac
C.Henry
B. of Siam
Malacca
St. of Malacca
Achem
I. of Hogs
Najas
E. Line
Sumatra I.
Bencoolen
I. of Good Fortune
Nassau
SUNDA
Engano
St. of Sunda
Borneo I.
Borneo
Sambas
Lava
Banjar
Madura
Java
Mataran
Batavia
Bantam
St. Clare
Mindanao I.
I. Dis. by Dampiere
St. Johanna
Sanguin
St. of Macassar
Celebes I.
Gilolo I.
SPICE Is.
Schouten
New Guinea
Banda Is.
Amboyna
Bura
Flores
Ombo
Timor
Letter
Arrou
New Holland
Balli
Lomboc
Cumbava
Sandelbosh
INDIAN OCEAN
Scale of Miles 60 to a D.
100 300 500 700 1000
165 L. E. from 175 Philad. 175 Lon. W. 165 155 145
10
0
10

EAST INDIA ISLANDS.

THE iſlands in the Indian Ocean are too numerous to admit of a deſcription here : We muſt therefore content ourſelves with mentioning only the moſt conſiderable of them.—BORNEO is the largeſt iſland in the world : It produces ſpices, wax, ſugar, tin, iron, gold, quickſilver, and the fineſt diamonds. There are ſeveral kings upon this iſland, who are unmoleſted by the Europeans. The Dutch only have ſome forts upon the coaſt, and are content with them, as long as they can thereby protect their trade. The moſt remarkable animal the iſland produces is the orang outang, a monkey as big as a man. Theſe people, like the inhabitants of ſome other of the Indian iſlands, ſhoot poiſoned darts at their enemies.—The MALDIVA iſlands, which are exceeding numerous, lie in one tract under the equator, and are moſt of them ſmall. The largeſt are the iſlands Male and Dive, and all theſe iſles are governed by one king, who reſides at Male. Notwithſtanding their ſituation, with reſpect to the equator, the air of theſe iſlands is very temperate, there falling a kind of dew every night, which greatly helps to qualify the heat, but is frequently mortal to ſtrangers.—The iſland of CEYLON abounds with ſpices, which the Dutch carry from thence to all parts of the word. The coaſt is well planted with groves of cinnamon-trees and cocoas, and no country abounds more with elephants. The Dutch have ſubdued all the coaſt, and ſuffer neither the king nor his ſubjects to have any intercourſe with other nations. The cinnamon-tree, which is peculiar to this iſland, is almoſt as valuable to the Dutch, as the mines

F   of

of Potofi are to the Spaniards. It is a vulgar error, that
cinnamon, nutmegs, mace, and cloves, grow all upon
one tree, or in one country; nutmegs grow only in
the Banda iflands, cloves only in the Molucca iflands,
and Amboyna, and the cinnamon, which is the bark of
a tree, only in Ceylon. The Molucca's, Banda, and
Amboyna, lie about 2000 miles to the eaftward of this
country.—SUMATRA lies near the Peninfula of Molucca. It produces rice, fugar, ginger, long-pepper, lemons, &c. there are alfo mines of lead, filver, and gold.
Their trade with the Europeans confifts chiefly in pepper, and both the Englifh and Dutch have feveral colonies here.—JAVA has feveral kings, but the Dutch are
here the moft powerful; and Batavia, which is an exceeding fine town and port, well fortified and defended
by a caftle and a ftrong garrifon, is the capital of all
the Dutch dominions in India. The manner in which
the Dutch got poffeffion of this ifland was as cruel and
inhuman as the conqueft of Mexico by the Spaniards.
—CELEBES and MOLUCCA lie both under the line.
They are fpice iflands, ufurped by the Dutch.—The
PHILIPPINE iflands lie moft of them in the Chinefe Ocean. The air of thefe iflands is wholefome, and the foil
produces plenty of all things neceffary for life. No
country in the world appears more beautiful, there
being a perpetual verdure : Buds, bloffoms, and fruit,
are feen upon the trees all the year round, as well on
the mountains as in the gardens that are cultivated;
but thefe iflands being hot and moift, produce abundance of venomous creatures, as the foil does poifon-
ous herbs and flowers.

RUSSIA in ASIA

NORTHERN OCEAN

C. Shelatshinskoi
C. Trisgalskoi
Kalima R.
Sea of Kants
zatka
Kants
Molotes
Indigar R.
Jana R.
SIBERIA
Yigma R.
Olekma R.
Witika R.
Lena R.
Aldan R.
M. for
Witim R.
Zakoti
Olentz R.
KINGDOM
Mivata Tungurka R.
Tungurka R.
Paykal
Nerchinski R.
Nevtschinski
Saghalian R.
EASTERN TARTARY
Tabl R.
Jenisea
Oczerezowa
Nerima
Jetinski
Tunski R.
Irkutzki R.
Kirangaro
Kangaro
Selenski
Kunetzi
Selinowski
Ob R.
Circle
TOBOLSKI
Tobolski
Jura
Koriski
Tungusi R.
Irtish R.
Sempalat
Weimofz
Stir
Nova Zemla
P. RUSSIA
Tobolski
P. Kim. of Tartar
Kusnetzoi
Astrachan
WESTERN TARTARY
White Sea
Onega
Samra
Astrachan

Scale of Miles
500   600   900
85 East From 60 London
70 Longitude

WESTERN TARTARY

RUSSIA IN ASIA.

THIS extensive country is situated between 40° and 135° east longitude, and between 53° and 72° north latitude, being bounded on the north by the Frozen Ocean; on the east, by the Pacific Ocean; on the south, by China, India, Persia, and the Caspian Sea ; and on the west, by European Russia.—The chief mountains are those of Caucasus in Circassia, and the mountains of Stolp in the north.—The principal rivers are the Wolga, the Obey, the Genesa, and the Lena.—The air in the north of Tartary is excessive cold, the earth being covered with snow nine months in the year. The southern provinces lie in a temperate climate; and would produce almost all manner of corn and vegetables, if there were hands to cultivate the soil; but those that inhabit it live a rambling vagrant life, driving great herds of cattle before them to such parts of the country where they can meet the best pasture, and seldom remain long enough in any one place to reap a crop of corn, if they should plough and sow the lands where they pitch their camps.—Their chief wild animals are rein-deer, elks, bears, foxes, ermines, and sables. There have been several rich mines of iron, copper, and silver, discovered in the north, and the iron works are very considerable. The country about Astracan is much improved by some French refugees, and other mechanics and husbandmen, whom the court of Russia sent thither.—The Tartars, as to stature, are generally thick and short, having flat faces, little eyes set deep in their heads, little round short noses, and an olive complexion. Their beards are
scarcely

RUSSIA IN ASIA.

scarcely visible, as they continually thin them by pulling the hairs up by the roots. They eat all manner of flesh but that of hogs, and delight most in horse-flesh; their usual drink is water. They are exceeding hospitable, and take a pleasure in entertaining strangers.—Most of the Asiatic Tartars inhabit the country now called Siberia. This extensive country was the ancient Scythia, and extends from the river Tabol to the Pacific Ocean, in it are multitudes of hords, or tribes, that have submitted to the Russian empire; of these the Calmucs are the most numerous. There are scarce any independent Tartar nations at present: Those of Thibet, and some of the Mogul Tartars, on the south-east, are almost the only people who acknowledge no superior.—The Usbec Tartars, which was the richest and most powerful of all the Tartar nations, were subdued by Kouli Kan, and made tributary to Persia. This country is situated in a very happy climate and fruitful soil, and carries on a very brisk trade between the eastern and western countries of Asia. This was the country of the victorious Tamerlane, who subdued most of the kingdoms of Asia, and some of his descendants were sovereigns of this country till very lately. Samarcand was the capital city in the reign of Tamerlane, but at present Bochara is the capital, which had a flourishing trade till it was plundered by Kouli Kan.—The Tartars of Cucallia, though generally considered as subject to Russia, are a very unsettled people, rambling from place to place, and owning themselves subject to any power that is most convenient for them.

CHINESE TARTARY

CHINA

COREA

Sea of Corea

EASTERN SEA

OR

SEA OF CHINA

Tropic of Cancer

Formosa I.

A Scale of Miles

Tartars

Yellow R.

Chinese Wall

Tibet K.

Pegu

Tonquin

Haynan I.

Lin-tin Shan

Longitude East from London

C H I N A.

THE empire of China is fituated between 95° and 135° eaſt longitude, and between 20° and 55° north latitude; being bounded on the north by Ruſſian Tartary; on the eaſt, by the Pacific Ocean, which divides it from North America; on the ſouth, by the Chineſian Sea; and on the weſt, by Tonquin and the Tartarian countries of Thibet and Ruſſia.—The moſt remarkable of their rivers, are, the Yamour, the Argun, the Croceus, the Kiam, and the Tay.—The air of this country is generally very temperate, except towards the north, where it is ſometimes intolerably cold, and that on account of ſeveral mountains of a prodigious height, whoſe tops are generally covered with ſnow. The ſoil is for the moſt part rich and fertile, inſomuch that the inhabitants are ſaid to have two, and ſometimes three harveſts in a year. It abounds with corn, wine, and all ſorts of fruits; its lakes and rivers are well furniſhed with fiſh, and ſome afford various kinds of pearls, and bezoar, of great value; its mountains, or more properly ſpeaking its hills, are richly lined with ſeveral mines of gold and ſilver, and its foreſts are every where ſtored with great plenty of veniſon. The tea-plant is peculiar to this country; of which they raiſe enough to furniſh the whole world: It degenerates when tranſplanted into another country, though it lies under the ſame latitude The green and the bohea are the ſame plant, but gathered at different ſeaſons, and differently cured, one by a natural heat, and the other by culinary fires: The bohea has ſome ingredi-ent mixed with it that gives it that yellowiſh caſt.--The

G emperor

CHINA.

emperor of China is abfolute, and his revenues amount
to more than the Great Mogul's —The Chinefe are of
a tolerable fair complexion, and have black hair. The
women are fmall, but extremely beautiful. The people in general are very courteous to ftrangers; but
they muft continue there for life, or depart quickly.
—Their chief manufactures are thofe of filk, cotton,
porcelain, cabinets, and lacquered ware. Their wrought
filks are inexpreffibly fine, and their gold and filver
ftuffs are not to be paralleled, any more than their
china-ware and cabinets; but, though their colours
are beautiful beyond imitation, their figures are pre-
pofterous and out of all fhape.—In this country are
feveral lakes remarkable for changing copper into
iron, at leaft fo in appearance. The great wall, which
feparates China from Tartary, is a very fingular curiofity : It begins in the province of Xenfi, which lies
on the north-weft of China, and is carried on over
mountains and vallies, and terminates at the Kang Sea,
between the provinces of Peking and Leaotom. The
whole courfe of it, with all the windings, Le Compte
tells us, is about 1500 miles. It is almoft all built of
brick, and of fuch well tempered mortar, that it has
now ftood near 2000 years, being built by the Emperor
Chiohampti, to prevent the incurfions of the Tartars,
and is very little decayed. It is about thirty feet high,
and broad enough for eight people to ride abreaft. It
is fortified all along with fquare towers, at the diftance
of a mile from each other. In this country is likewife
a large mountain full of terrible caverns, in one of
which is a lake of fuch a nature, that if a ftone be
thrown into it, there is prefently heard a hideous noife,
as of a frightful clap of thunder.

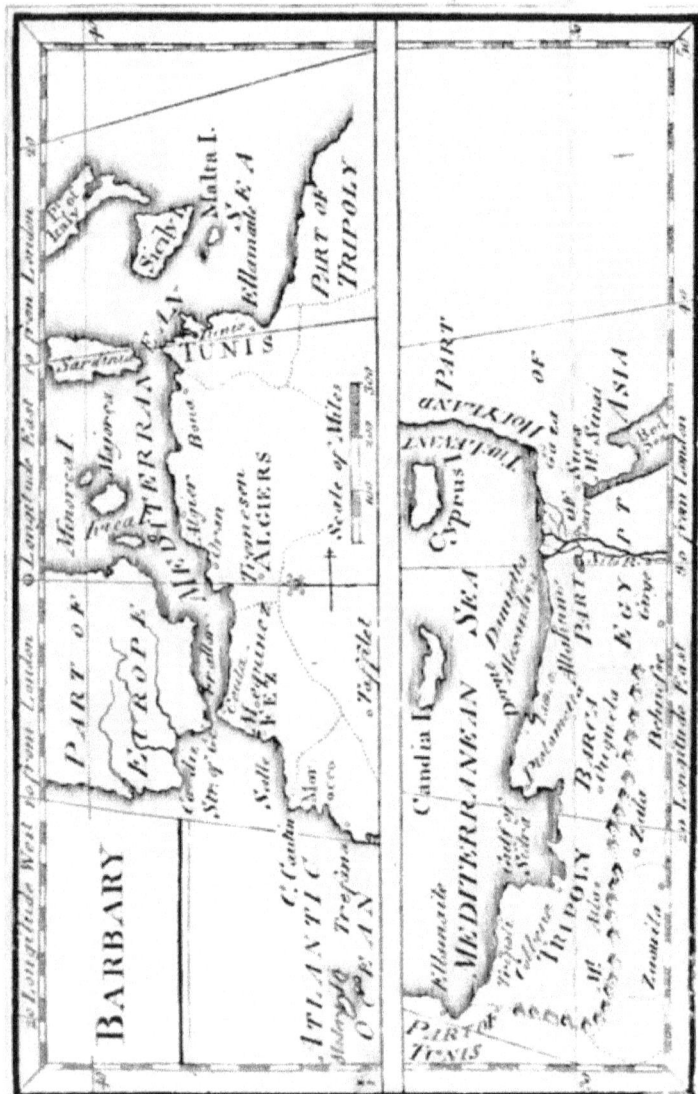

BARBARY.

BARBARY extends from the straits of Gibraltar to the river Nile, and is parted from Europe by the Mediterranean Sea.—MOROCCO and FEZ have each a capital of the same name, and of these the latter is the richest city in all Barbary : Here is the residence of the emperor of Morocco. Tangier is a strong fortification, formerly in the possession of the English, who left it, after having demolished it, in 1685.—The republic of ALGIERS, which lies along the Mediterranean, has likewise a capital of its own name, and is surrounded by a wall twelve feet thick, and thirty feet high. In 1688, it was terribly bombarded by the French. The Algerines are reckoned the richest and most noted rovers in Africa, and it is said that no place in the world possesses so much specie. They are in general a cruel, treacherous, and covetous people.—TUNIS was formerly called *Terra Punica,* wherein Carthage was the capital. It was governed by their own kings, but is now a republic belonging to the Turks. Tunis it the capital, which has a strong castle upon an eminence. In the old palace is kept the Divan, wherein also resides the Dey.—The kingdom of TRIPOLI lies along the Mediterranean, wherein is Tripoli, the capital, which, though not very large, is populous. The government of this country, as well as that of Tunis, is regulated by a divan, or common-council, of which the Dey is president.—Near to this is the kingdom of BARCA, which is a poor country, wanting springs, and little else thrives there than dates. This country, with Egypt, fell into the hands of the Turks, and is govern-

ed

BARBARY.

ed by a bafha, who refides at Tripoli.—Mount Atlas runs the whole length of Barbary, and borders upon that ocean which divides the eaftern from the weftern continent, and is from this mountain called the Atlantic Ocean. The poets feigned that this mountain fuftained the univerfe, from whence we fee Atlas reprefented with the world upon his fhoulders; and every defcription of a globe affumes the name of an Atlas: Hence *Atlas Minimus*, the title of this volume.—The air of this country is for the moft part temperate, and generally efteemed very healthful. The foil, in moft places, is fertile in corn, and moft kinds of fruit, though it is full of mountains and forefts, efpecially towards the Mediterranean Sea. It breeds vaft numbers of lions, leopards, apes, and elephants, which, with the gangs of robbers that frequent the roads, make travelling here very dangerous. When they traverfe their extenfive deferts, they are forced to load one half of their camels with water, to prevent their perifhing with drought; but there is ftill a more dangerous enemy, and that is the fand itfelf. When the wind rifes, the caravan is perfectly covered with the duft, and there have been inftances, both in Africa and Afia, where whole caravans, and even armies, have been buried alive in the fands. There are likewife hot winds, which blow over a long tract of burning fand, equal almoft to the heat of an oven, which deftroy great numbers of merchants and pilgrims.—Very few manufactures are encouraged in Barbary; they are partly fupplied by their own buccaniers, and the reft of their wants are relieved by Jew merchants, who brave the barbarifm of the country, for the advantages they derive from trading in it.

NEGROLAND and GUINEA

NEGROLAND

DESERT

P.ᵗ of SAARA or THE

ATLANTIC OCEAN

Kingdom of Benin

Gold Coast

Tooth Coast

Grain Coast

Slave Coast

A Scale of Miles

Longitude West from London

Longᵗ E. from London

NEGROLAND AND GUINEA.

THESE countries are bounded on the north by part of Sierra, or the Defert; on the eaft, by the unknown parts of Africa; and on the fouth and weft by the Atlantic Ocean.—The mountains of Sierra Leon are the moft remarkable.—The principal rivers are thofe of Coanzo, Zaara, Lunde, Cameron, Formofa, and Niger, befides feveral others of lefs note; but few of them are navigable for any confiderable length, defcending precipitately from high mountains, and running but fhort courfes before they fall into the fea, excepting the Niger, up which the Englifh have failed 500 miles, and have factories on both fhores.—At the fhifting of the equinoxes they have violent ftorms of wind, with terrible thunder and lightning.—As every part of Guinea lies between the two tropics, the air is exceffive hot, and the flat country, being overflowed great part of the year by the periodical rains, is confequently unwholefome. This is not the cafe, however, with Negroland, where the air, though warm, is efteemed very wholefome. The foil is rich, and here are great ftore of cattle and corn, and variety of herbs, as alfo fome mines of gold and filver. In Guinea they have no wheat, but plenty of Guinea grain, rice, maize, or Indian corn. Here are no grapes; but the palm-tree affords them wine, and the cocoa-nut a pleafant drink : Here are alfo oranges and lemons, pomegranates, pineapples, and other tropical fruits.—Their minerals are gold, copper, and iron. The Portuguefe poffefs the fouthern coaft of Congo, Angola, &c. but in that part, which is called Guinea Proper, the Englifh, Dutch, French and other nations, have their feveral colonies

H   and

and settlements. In Guinea there are some sovereign princes whose dominions are very extensive, rich, and powerful; they are arbitrary monarchs, limited by no laws, and strangers to restraint. Besides these, there are a multitude of others, whose dominions do not exceed the bounds of an ordinary parish, and whose power and revenues are proportionably mean, arising chiefly from a continual petty warfare kept up for the express purpose of kidnapping and selling to the European traders every human being they can seize from each other. These unhappy wretches forfeit, with their liberty, every right of human nature; they hold, when in the West India islands, their conjugal, paternal, and filial engagements at the will and pleasure of fellow men, who call themselves their OWNERS !!! The English have the guilty pre-eminence in this nefarious and most execrable traffic; however, it is not now a *national iniquity*; the voice of the people has loudly expressed their general detestation of it : The natives, descended from the original inhabitants, are all negroes, well known by their flat noses, thick lips, and short woolly hair.—The habit of the common people, in Proper Guinea, is a cloth about their middle; but people of condition have another over their shoulders, and are adorned with abundance of rings and bracelets. The arms, legs and great part of the bodies of the men are naked; but the women are veiled when they go abroad. The habit of the common people in Negroland is not very different from that of Proper Guinea; but their chiefs and people of condition are clothed in white vests, with white caps on their heads, and these, their complexion being exceeding black, make a pretty appearance. The negroes live but very poorly.

EGYPT,
NUBIA
and
ABISSINIA.

W. Barker. sculp.

Cyprus I.

LEVANT

Alexandria

Gama

CAIRO

Avla

M.t Sinai

EGYPT

Girge

Suez

Cosir

PART

of

Behnes

Armand

Gr. Cataract

Medina

Tropic of Cancer

Meeho

Ibrim

Komel

NUBIA

Dongola

RED SEA

Mecca

ASIA

ARABIA

H. Cataract

White R.

Deren

Dabarua

Arkio

Dhafar

Seunar

Tacra R.

Sini

Mocha

Adel

Makulla

L. of

Dambea

Mina

Abeta

Sana

K. of Tigra

Babelmandel

ABISSINIA

Zeila

ADEL

K. of Galles

C. Rasalgat

Nuleo R.

Sangara

Bocha

Gingiro

AJAN

Magadoxa

Scale of Miles.

100   500   600

Lon. E. from   40   London

EGYPT, NUBIA, AND ABYSSINIA.

THESE extensive countries are situated between 30° and 36° east longitude, and between 5° and 32° north latitude, being bounded by the Levant Sea on the north, by part of Asia on the east, by the lower Ethiopia on the south, and by the desart of Barca and the unknown parts of Africa, on the west.—The air of Egypt is very hot, and generally esteemed extremely unwholesome, being infested with nauseous vapours which ascend from the fat and slimy soil of the earth; but this must be understood only of that time in which the waters are low; for the Nile no sooner begins to rise and overflow its banks, than all distempers cease. The air of Nubia is very hot in the day-time, but cool in the night; and that of Abyssinia, or Upper Ethiopia, lying very little north of the line, is sultry hot.— The soil of Egypt, as far as the flood extends, has been formed by the mud which the Nile carries with it. As soon as the waters retire, the husbandman has little more to do than to harrow his corn and other seed in the mud, and is sometimes obliged to temper the mud with sand, to prevent the corn being too rank. In a month or two afterwards, the fields are covered with all manner of grain, peas, and beans, and other pulse, and where grain is not sown, their grazing grounds become rich pastures. The lower Egypt is all a sea at the height of the flood, and only the tops of the forests and fruit-trees appear, intermixed with towns and villages built upon natural or artificial hills; in the **dry** seasons are seen beautiful gardens, corn-fields, and meadows, well stocked with flocks and herds. The common

mon people live part of the year on cucumbers, and find no manner of inconvenience from that kind of food.—The modern Egyptians are generally reckoned cowardly and luxurious, cruel, cunning, and treacherous: They are much degenerated from their ancestors in every thing, except a vain affectation of divining, which some still pretend to.—This country (very famous of old both in sacred and profane history) being now a province of the Turkish empire, is governed by a Bashaw, who commonly resides at Grand Cairo, which post is generally considered as the most honourable government of any belonging to the Porte, having under him no less than fifteen governments, as also a powerful militia.—The kingdom of NUBIA lies along the Nile, between Egypt and Abyssinia. It has a capital of the same name, which is the residence of the king, and is very large. The houses are but one story high, and covered with turf and stone to keep off the heat of the sun.—Nubia is governed by its own independent king, who is said to be a very powerful prince. —ABYSSINIA is also called the Upper Ethiopia, or the country of the Moors. According to the account the Portuguese give of this country, it contains thirty kingdoms, besides twenty-two more which lie about it, and belonged formerly to Abyssinia, but now are governed by their own kings.—This large country is governed by their sovereign king, whose subjects are treated like slaves; and he is held in such veneration among them, that at his very name they bow their bodies, and touch the ground with one of their fingers. The natives are coal-black, and travellers give them the character of a brisk, sensible, and civil people, and great lovers of learned men.

Long. E. 15 from Phila

A Scale of Miles 60 to a Degree

600 500 400 300 200 100

Equinoctial Line

Great River.

Nova Caya
Para
Camutá

Pt. OF

A M A

ZONIA

St. Louis de
Moranham

St. Maria

Tupinambas a famous
Nation who inhabited
Brasil on its first
discovery.

Most of this Inland
is Unknown the Na-
tives bear the gene-
ral Name of Ta-
payos.

A Space of Fifty
Thousand
Square Leagues

This Country
abounds with small Rivers

Pt. OF

PARA

GUAY

St. Paul

St. Santos

Aranacari

St. Catharine

Patos

St. Peter

Rio Plata

Tortuga P.
Baxos or Sandy I.

Seara

A Village of
Salt works

Paraiba
Olinda or
Pernambuc

Tamarical

THE

Oregippi
del Rey
Terra d'avila

Salvador
of all Saints
Leos Ilheo

WESTERN

Baxos
Abrollos

Spiritu Santo

C. St. Thomas

OCEAN

Cape Frio

Janeiro R.
Ilha grand

Tropic of Capricorn

BRASIL

J. Roche Sct.

B R A S I L.

THE dominions of Portugal in South America are called Brafil, and are fituated between 35° and 60° weft longitude, and between the equator and 35° fouth latitude. It is bounded by the mouth of the river Amazon, and the Atlantic Ocean, on the north; by the fame ocean, on the eaft; by the mouth of the river Plata, on the fouth; and by a chain of mountains, which divide it from Spanifh America, and the country of Amazons, on the weft. The climate of this country, towards the northward, is uncertain, hot, boifterous, and unwholefome: The country, there, and even in more temperate parts, is annually overflowed; but to the fouthward, beyond the tropic of Capricorn, there is no part of the world that enjoys a more ferene and wholefome air, refrefhed with the foft breezes of the ocean on one hand, and the cool air of the mountains on the other. Hither feveral aged people from Portugal retire for their health, and protract their lives to a long and eafy age. In general, the foil is extremely fruitful, and was found very fufficient for the comfortable fubfiftence of the inhabitants, till the mines of gold and diamonds were difcovered. Thefe, with the fugar plantations, occupy fo many hands, that agriculture lies neglected; and confequently Brazil depends upon Europe for its daily bread. The chief commodities which this country yields for a foreign market, are fugar, tobacco, hides, indigo, ipecacuanha, balfam of copaibo, and Brazil wood. The trade of Brazil is very great, and is encreafing every year: It is the richeft, moft flourifhing, and moft growing eftablifhment in

BRASIL.

all America.--The Portuguese in this part of the world
are represented as a people at once sunk in the most
effeminate luxury, and practising the most desperate
crimes; of a dissembling, hypocritical temper; of little
honesty in dealing, or sincerity in conversation: lazy,
proud, and cruel; they are poor, and penurious in their
diet, not more through necessity than inclination; for,
like the inhabitants of most southern climates, they are
much more fond of show, state, and attendants, than of
the joys of free society, and the satisfaction of a good
table; yet their feasts, seldom made, are sumptuous to
extravagance. However, the inhabitants of the Rio de
Janeiro, and in the northern captainships, are not near so
effeminate and corrupted as those of the Bay of All Saints,
which, being in a climate favourable to indolence and
debauchery, the capital city, and one of the oldest settlements, is, in all respects, worse than any of the
other.----The government of Brasil is in the viceroy,
who resides at St. Salvador: He has two councils, one
for criminal, the other for civil affairs, in both which
he presides; but, to the infinite prejudice of the settle-
ment, all the delay, chicanery, and multiplied expences,
incident to the worst part of the law, and practised by the
most corrupted lawyers, flourish here, at the same time
that justice is so lax, that the greatest crimes often pass
with impunity. Upon the river Amazons, the people, who
are mostly Indians, and reduced by the priests sent thither, are still under the government of these pastors.---
The Indians are of a good stature, and as they inhabit a
hot climate almost under the equator, are of a dark copper
colour, their hair black, and hanging over their shoulders.
Their ornaments are glittering stones hung upon their lips
or nostrils, and bracelets of feathers about their arms.

THE WESTERN OCEAN

BRASIL

AMAZONIA

PARAGUAY

Parana

River

Paraguay

Parana

Rio Plata

C. St Anthony

THE SOUTH SEA

PERU

Tropic of Capricorn

EL CHACO

TUCUMAN

CHILI

½ Long. E. 15 from Phil. ro Iam.

PARAGUAY.
and
TUCUMAN

J. Roche &c.

A Scale of Miles 60 to a Degree

PARAGUAY and TUCUMAN.

THESE countries are situated between 50° and 70° west longitude, and between 20° and 37° south latitude, being bounded by Amazonia on the north, by Brasil on the east, by Patagonia on the south, and by Peru and Chili on the west.----This vast territory is far from being wholly subdued or planted by the Spaniards; there are many parts in a great degree unknown to them, or to any other people of Europe. In such a vast country, which lies in climes so different, we must expect to meet with great diversity of soil and product. In general, however, this country is fertile; the pastures, in particular, are so rich, that they are covered with innumerable herds of black cattle, horses, and mules, in which hardly any one thinks it worth his while to claim a property, they being so plenty as to render them an article in common.---The principal province in this vast tract is Rio de la Plata, being so called from the very extensive river of that name. This province, with all the adjacent parts, is one continued level, uninterrupted by the least hill for several hundreds of miles every way, extremely fertile in most things; but contrary to the general nature of America, destitute of woods: This want they endeavour to supply by plantations of every kind of fruit trees, all which thrive here to admiration.—— The air is remarkably sweet and serene, and the waters of the great river La Plata are equally pure and wholesome: They annually overflow their banks, and, on their recess, leave the land enriched with a slime, which produces the greatest quantity of whatever is committed to it.——The principal town is Buenos Ayres,

on

PARAGUAY and TUCUMAN.

on the fouth fide of the river: This town is the only place of traffic to the fouthward of Brafil; yet its trade, confidering the rich and extenfive country to which it is the avenue, is very inconfiderable.—We muft not quit Paraguay without faying fomething of that extraordinary fpecies of commonwealth which the Jefuits have erected in the interior parts. About the middle of the laft century, the Jefuits, by permiffion of the court of Madrid, entered upon this defign. They began by gathering together about fifty wandering families, whom they perfuaded to fettle, and they united them into a little townfhip. This was the flight foundation upon which they have built a fuperftructure that amazed the world. It is faid, that, from fuch inconfiderable beginnings, feveral years ago, their fubjects amounted to 300,000 families. They lived in towns, very regularly clad, laboured in agriculture, and exercifed manufactures; fome even afpired to the elegant arts: They were inftructed in the military with the moft exact difcipline, and could raife 60,000 men well armed. To effect thefe purpofes, they, from time to time, brought over from Europe feveral handicraftfmen, muficians, painters, &c. On their firft fettlement, the governors of the adjacent provinces had orders from Madrid not to interfere, nor to fuffer any Spaniard to enter their pale without licence from the fathers. They, on their part, agreed to pay a certain capitation tax, in proportion to their flock, and to fend a certain number to the king's works whenever they fhould be demanded, and they be able to fupply them.

Long: E. & from Phila

A Scale of Miles 60 to a Degree

600 500 400 300 200 100

TERRA FIRMA

Emeraldas Equinoctial Line R. Negro

Tacungo Quito R. Yupura

Guayaquil Elga

Bay of Cuenza St Ignacio River Amazon

Guayaquil de Pevas AMAZONIA

Borja

Payta Laguna

Moyobamba

Casamarco Lamas

Truxillo Guanuco

Tarma Lima

THE Pisco Cusco

St Juan Port Yanaca This Wide

SOUTH Chiquito Region abounds

Arequipa with Tribes of

SEA Moquegua Cruz people who are

Arica little known.

Caravache Chuquisaca PARAGU

Atacama

Lipez Tropic of Capricorn

TUCUMAN

Bay de Nostra

PERU Senora

J. Roche Sc.

P E R U.

THIS part of South America is fituated between 60° and 81° weft longitude, and between the equator and 25° fouth latitude, being bounded by Terra Firma on the north, by Amazonia on the eaft, by Chili on the fouth, and by the South Sea or the Pacific Ocean on the weft —About thirty miles within land is a chain of mountains called the Sierras; and beyond thefe, about eighty miles, are prodigious high mountains, called the Cordeleras des Andes, which, with the Sierras, run the whole length of South America, upwards of 3000 miles. Acofta relates, that endeavouring to pafs thefe mountains with a great many other people, they were all taken with fuch reachings to vomit, that they expected every moment to be their laft ; for not only green phlegm and choler came up, but a great deal of blood ; and that it lafted for three or four hours, till they had defcended to the lower part of the hill, when this ficknefs went off without being attended with any ill confequences. The air was fo fubtile and piercing, that it penetrated the entrails not only of man but of beafts, being almoft too much rarified for animals to breathe in: And hence it is, that there are no beafts upon them, either wild or tame. The Spaniards formerly paffed thefe mountains in their way to Chili ; but now they either go by fea, or by the fide of thefe mountains to avoid the danger, fo many have perifhed in going over them; and others, who have efcaped with their lives, have loft their fingers and toes, and been otherwife lamed. Acofta fays, he was informed by General Coftilla, who had loft three or four fingers in croffing them in his way

K 2

PERU.

to Chili, that they fell off without any pain ; and that
the fame general, marching over them once with an
army, great part of his men fuddenly fell down dead,
whofe bodies were fome time afterwards feen lying
on the fpot, without any appearance of decay, ftench,
or putrefaction.— It never rains in that part of the
country which lies near the fea coaft, unlefs within
three or four degrees of the equator; but the country
is watered by the rivers which fall from the Andes
into the South Seas: Thefe they turn into their fields
and gardens, and have their vintage and harveft at
what time of the year they pleafe, this being the
only country between the tropics that affords wine.—
The commodities of Peru are filver and gold, wine,
oil, brandy, wool, jefuit's bark, and Guinea or Jamaica pepper.—Quickfilver is peculiar to this part of
America, it not having yet been found that it is any
where elfe produced on this continent.—The manners of the Spaniards and Creolians of Peru refemble,
with little difference, thofe of Mexico, except that
the natives of Peru feem to be of a more liberal turn
and of greater ingenuity ; but they are for the moft
part, equally deftitute of all cultivation. The flavery
of the Indians here is almoft beyond defcription or
belief.—There are three cities in Peru, famous for
their opulence and trade: Lima, Cufco, and Quito.—
Lima lies in the northern part of Peru, and ftands about
two leagues from the fea, upon a river called Nimac,
fmall and unnavigable. This city is the capital of
Peru, and of all South America: It extends in length
about two miles, and in breadth about one and a
quarter. The houfes are built low, and of light materials, to avoid the confequences of earthquakes, fre-

quent

CHILI.

quent and dreadful in this country. Lima has 54 churches, 13 monafteries, 6 colleges of jefuits, 12 nunneries, and as many hofpitals, befides foundations for the portioning of poor girls. In 1747, a moft terrible earthquake entirely devoured Callao, the port belonging to Lima, and laid three fourths of the city level to the ground. The deftruction of Callao was the moft fudden and terrible that can be conceived, no more than one of the inhabitants efcaping, and he by a providence the moft fingular and extraordinary imaginable. This man was on the fort that overlooked the harbour, and was going to ftrike the flag, when he perceived the fea retire a confiderable diftance, and then fwelling mountains high, it returned with great violence. The inhabitants ran from their houfes in the utmoft terror and confufion. He heard a cry of *Miferere* rife from all parts of the city, and immediately all was filent: The fea had entirely overwhelmed the city, and buried it for ever in its bofom; but the fame wave which deftroyed the city, drove a little Boat by the place where the man ftood, into which he threw himfelf and was faved. Whilft this town fubfifted, it contained about 3000 inhabitants of all kinds, and poffeffed the fineft port in all Peru. —*Cufco*, the capital of the ancient empire, fituated in the mountainous part of the country, is ftill a very confiderable city, and the inhabitants, who are three parts of them Indians, are very induftrious and ingenious.---*Quito* is likewife an inland town, fituated in the northern part of Peru, and is a very confiderable and populous place.

Immediately to the fouthward of Peru lies CHILI, extending itfelf in a long narrow flip, over the coaft of the South Sea, in the fouth temperate zone. The

air

PATAGONIA.

air here is remarkably clear and ferene: Scarce any
changes happen for three parts of the year, and very
little rain falls during that period; but the benign
dews every night, and the many rivulets with which
the neighbourhood of the Andes fupplies them, fer-
tilize the plain country, and make it produce as much
corn, wine, oil, and fruits, as the fmall number of
inhabitants can confume, or their induftry, which is
but moderate, will fuffer them to raife. If it were
under a more favourable government, and better peopled, there is hardly any part of the world which
could enter into competition with this. Chili has but
very few beafts of prey ; and though toads, fnakes,
and fcorpions, are here as numerous as in other hot
countries, they are found entirely harmlefs. There
are in Chili four towns of fome note, either on the
fea or near it ; St. Jago, which is the capital, and
contains about 4000 families; La Conception, Co-
quimbo or La Serena, and Baldivia.

To the fouth of Chili is PATAGONIA, as may be
feen in the map of South America. It is a mountainous
country, covered with fnow great part of the year, and
confequently exceffively cold; nor is it much cultivated by
the natives, who live chiefly upon fifh and game, and
what the earth fpontaneoufly produces. The Patagonians
live in thatched huts, and wear no clothes, notwithfland-
ing the rigour of the climate, except a mantle made of
feal-fkin, or the fkin of fome beaft, which they throw
off when they are in action. Many of them are of a
gigantic ftature, near nine feet in height, as we are
affured by Mr. Clarke, who accompanied Commodore
Byron in his voyage to the ftraits of Magellan in the
year 1764. It however appears, from other relations,
that

PATAGONIA.

that b....s the above gigantic inhabitants, there are
...ers of moderate stature, like those of the rest of the
globe. The complexions of both are tawny, and their
hair black ; but they paint their faces and bodies with
several colours. They are a brave, hardy race, very active,
and head their arms, bows and arrows, with flints. They
have canoes and boats made of a tree hollowed ; and
their nets are made of the fibres of the bark of trees, or
of the guts or sinews of animals. The principal strait in
this part is that of Magellan, which separates the continent from Terra del Fuego. About the middle of this
strait is a promontory, called Cape Froward, which is the
most southerly land on the continent of South America ;
for Terra del Fuego is properly an island, being divided
from the continent by this narrow strait. The Spaniards,
who built a fort upon the straits of Magellan, and left a
garrison in it, to prevent any other European nations from
passing that way into the South Seas, lost most of their
men, who perished for want of food ; from whence that
place obtained the name of Port Famine, and no people
have since attempted to plant colonies there.

LATE DISCOVERIES.

THE British ships employed in exploring unknown
regions, have penetrated into the most obscure
parts of the South Pacific Ocean ; have visited the
most material discoveries of former navigators, and in
repeatedly traversing that sea within the southern
tropic, have made many new ones, have found a pro-
fusion of habitable and inhabited islands, interspersed
through the amazing space of fourscore degrees of
longitude, either separately scattered or grouped in
numerous clusters; of them and their inhabitants
very ample accounts have been given us.

LATE DISCOVERIES.

The foremost in name and merit among the benefactors of mankind is Captain Cook. Perhaps few individuals have added more to any one science than this great man has done to geography. In his first voyage, he discovered the Society Islands, ascertained the insularity of New Zealand, and discovered the straits which separate the two islands, and are called after his name; he explored the eastern coast of New Holland, till then unknown, an extent of twenty-seven degrees of latitude, and upwards of two thousand miles.

He gave, in his second expedition, a solution to the great problem of a southern continent; having so completely traversed that hemisphere, as not to leave a possibility of its existence, unless it is so near the pole as to be beyond the reach of navigation. New Caledonia, the largest island in the southern Pacific, except New Zealand, was discovered in this voyage: Also the Island of Georgia; and an unknown coast, which the Captain named Sandwich Land; and having twice visited the tropical seas, he settled the situations of the old, and made several new discoveries.

In his third and last voyage, he discovered the Sandwich Islands; which, on account of their situation and productions, may perhaps become an object of more consequence than any other discovery in the South Sea; he explored what had before remained unknown of the western coast of America, an extent of three thousand seven hundred miles; ascertained the proximity of the two continents of Asia and America; sailed through the straits between them, and surveyed the coasts on each side, so far as to be satisfied of the impracticability of a passage in that hemisphere, from the Atlantic into the Pacific Ocean, by an eastern or western course.

FINIS.